2002

PERSONAL IDENTITY

A Philosophical Analysis

ALSO BY GODFREY VESEY

Body and Mind (ed.), 1964
The Embodied Mind, 1965
The Human Agent (ed.), 1968
Talk of God (ed.), 1969
Knowledge and Necessity (ed.), 1970
Perception, 1970
The Proper Study (ed.), 1971
Reason and Reality (ed.), 1972
Philosophy and the Arts (ed.), 1973
Understanding Wittgenstein (ed.), 1974
   (Cornell Paperback, 1976)
Philosophy in the Open (ed.), 1974
Impressions of Empiricism (ed.), 1976

PERSONAL IDENTITY

A Philosophical Analysis

GODFREY VESEY

Cornell Paperbacks

Cornell University Press

ITHACA, NEW YORK

First printing, Cornell Paperbacks, 1977

International Standard Book Number 0–8014–9162–2
Library of Congress Catalog Card Number 76–41208
Printed in the United States of America
*Librarians: Library of Congress cataloging information appears
on the last page of the book.*

CONTENTS

ACKNOWLEDGEMENTS

In 1966 I read a paper entitled 'Personal Identity and the Co-personality of Experiences' at a number of universities in America and England. I am grateful to Frank Ebersole and Terry Penelhum, in America, and to Bernard Williams and Richard Wollheim, in England, for their comments on it. Dan O'Connor and Hywel Lewis, and three of my colleagues at The Open University, John Ferguson, Ossie Hanfling and Peter Lewis, read the first draft of the book, based on the paper. That the final draft is several chapters shorter than the first is some indication of my indebtedness to them.

PERSONAL IDENTITY

A Philosophical Analysis

1. IN WHICH A LABYRINTH IS EXPLORED AND LANDMARKS ESTABLISHED

(i) HUME'S 'LABYRINTH' . . .

'Problems', in philosophy, are states of perplexity into which philosophers get – often as a result of their own well-intentioned efforts to correct the mistakes of other philosophers. Refreshingly, they sometimes admit to being bewildered, and to not knowing what can have gone wrong in their thinking about some matter. Let us begin with just such an admission. It is by the British empiricist philosopher David Hume. I do not think the terminology in which he formulated his problem is particularly conducive to finding a solution, but before we start clarifying – drawing distinctions, and so on – let us see what it is that has to be clarified.

In outline, the situation is this. Hume asked himself 'whether in pronouncing concerning the identity of a person, we observe some real bond among his perceptions, or only feel one among the ideas we form of them' (42, p. 259).* In the body of his *Treatise of Human Nature* he described how this question arises, and worked out his own answer to it, using what he regarded as sound empiricist principles. But it was an answer about

* Numerals in parentheses refer to works numerically listed in the Bibliography on pp. 115–23.

which he came to have profound misgivings. In the Appendix he wrote: 'Upon a more strict review of the section concerning *personal identity*, I find myself involv'd in such a labyrinth, that, I must confess, I neither know how to correct my former opinions, nor how to render them consistent' (42, p. 633). Let us explore Hume's 'labyrinth'.

(ii) . . . EXPLORED

On the face of it, Hume's question seems anything but a sensible one to ask. It is about what we observe 'in pronouncing concerning the identity of a person', but both the answers between which one is invited to choose involve observing someone's *perceptions*. How does one observe another person's perceptions? Presumably by asking him about them. But then we must already have decided which person to ask. That is, we must have identified a person in some way other than by reference to perceptions. If he is someone we know, we will have identified him by looking, or perhaps by hearing his voice. If not, we may have asked him who he is, or asked someone else who he is. But having identified him in this way what is the point of enquiring about his perceptions?

This is so obvious that Hume could hardly have failed to realise it. What, then, did he mean by the question about 'the identity of a person'? The answer is provided by the following passage, from the Appendix:

> Most philosophers seem inclin'd to think, that personal identity *arises* from consciousness;

and consciousness is nothing but a reflected thought or perception. The present philosophy, therefore, has so far a promising aspect. But all my hopes vanish, when I come to explain the principles, that unite our successive perceptions in our thought or consciousness. I cannot discover any theory, which gives me satisfaction on this head. (42, pp. 635–6)

The question about 'the identity of a person' is evidently, for Hume, a question about how our successive perceptions are 'united'. Are they *really* united, or does it merely *feel* as if they are united? And if the latter, what explains the feeling?

But it is still not clear what is being asked. What lies behind the question about perceptions being 'united'? The question comes up, Hume implies, if the view is taken that 'personal identity *arises* from consciousness'. What would it be for it *not* to arise from consciousness? What is the view that most philosophers would *reject*, the view that only some would accept?

The section on personal identity begins as follows:

There are some philosophers, who imagine we are every moment intimately conscious of what we call our SELF; that we feel its existence and its continuance in existence; and are certain, beyond the evidence of a demonstration, both of its perfect identity and simplicity. (42, p. 251)

The idea seems to be that if only we were conscious of our self then it would be clear why we think of ourselves as in some sense remaining the same throughout the succession of experiences that make up our lives. My consciousness of my self would explain my having an idea of my personal identity throughout the changes in my life-history. But Hume cannot admit that we are conscious of our self. Why not? He invokes the empiricist principle that all real ideas are derived from 'some one impression', notes that 'self or person is not any one impression, but that to which our several impressions and ideas are suppos'd to have a reference', and concludes that the question 'From what impression is the idea of self derived?' cannot be answered 'without a manifest contradiction and absurdity' (42, p. 251).

So far, so good. But Hume risks confusing the reader at this point by going straight on to state an objection to a *different* theory. This is the theory that we could derive the idea of self not from an impression of self (impossible because of what the self is) but from *any* impression, provided it continued 'invariably the same, thro' the whole course of our lives'. It would have to do this 'since self is suppos'd to exist after that manner'. Hume's objection to this is that 'there is no impression constant and invariable'.

If the idea of self is not derived from an impression of self (impossible because of what the self is), and not derived from any other impression (impossible because there is not an impression with the required longevity, etc.), what follows? Evidently, that we have no real (i.e. impression-derived) idea of self. But if it is not the case that perceptions are connected with one another because they are connected with one continuing real idea of self, how are they connected? 'They are distinct existences, and the mind never perceives any real connexion among distinct existences' (42, p. 636). Therefore there is no real connexion between them. And yet we think of them as being connected. There is what Hume calls a 'felt bond' among a person's perceptions, and, corresponding to it, a 'fictitious' idea of self. In that case, how does the bond come to be felt?

Hume's answer is in terms of the relations that exist between a person's perceptions. They may be related in any of three ways: resemblance, contiguity, and causation. Contiguity, he decides, 'has little or no influence in the present case'. That leaves resemblance and causation. If we were unable to forget anything, then, since memory is 'a faculty by which we raise up images of past perceptions' and since 'an image necessarily resembles its object', there would be a great deal of resemblance in 'the train of perceptions'. But we do forget things, so resemblance cannot be the relation that makes the different perceptions 'seem like the continuance of one object'. The only remaining possibility is causation:

> The true idea of the human mind, is to consider it as a system of different perceptions or different existences, which are link'd together by the relation of cause and effect, and

> mutually produce, destroy, influence, and modify each other. (42, p. 261)

One way of expressing Hume's theory would be to say that if he were asked 'Does the fact that two perceptions are the same person's perceptions explain their being causally linked, or does the fact that they are causally linked explain their being the same person's perceptions?' he would have to say the latter.

No wonder he described the position in which he found himself as a 'labyrinth'.

(iii) ESTABLISHING LANDMARKS: THE UNITY QUESTION . . .

Having seen what the labyrinth is like, let us try to establish some landmarks.

One that is obviously called for is a clarification of the distinction between the question, whatever it is, with which Hume and the philosophers to whom he refers (the many who 'seem inclin'd to think, that personal identity *arises* from consciousness' and the few who 'imagine we are every moment intimately conscious of what we call our SELF') are concerned, and the question as to how we ordinarily do, or should, settle disputes about who is who.

I think this can best be achieved by formulating two questions, which I shall call the 'Unity Question' and the 'Identity Question'. The Unity Question is such that in answering it we can discuss a good many of the positions Hume could

not accept, including his own, and also one or two
that never occurred to him. It goes like this:

The Unity Question

> In his lifetime a person has many sensa-
> tions, feelings, emotions, thoughts, mem-
> ories, and so on. All these experiences
> have one thing in common: they are all
> *his* experiences, they are all in *his* mind.
> But what is it for different experiences to
> have this in common? What *unites* a per-
> son's present experiences with his past
> experiences? Is it a matter of their all
> being related to one and the same self-
> conscious self, or of their all being
> related to one and the same continuing
> experience which acts as a sort of back-
> ground to them, or of their all being
> related to each other in some way, or
> what? What is the principle of unity?

You will notice that there are aspects of Hume's
question that are not reproduced in this question;
for instance, the part about ideas being derived
from impressions, and about some of our ideas
being real and others fictitious. Never mind. You
will find that the Unity Question, and the answers
to it, are quite enough to be getting on with.

(iv) . . . AND THE IDENTITY QUESTION

Having formulated the Unity Question now let us
have the Identity Question. This is it:

The Identity Question

> We normally identify people in a variety
> of ways, but primarily by their physical
> appearance. On the telephone we can
> sometimes identify them if they say no
> more than 'Hello'. The police have more
> specialised techniques, such as taking
> people's fingerprints. Usually, of course,
> the different ways of identifying people
> do not lead to disagreement as to who
> someone is. But it is not difficult to
> imagine problem cases. Suppose, for
> instance, that Brown's brain is trans-
> planted into Robinson's body. Is the
> resulting person Brown or Robinson?
> In general, what is essential to personal
> identity?

This question is one which a reflective person can
hardly fail to ask himself if he reads science
fiction stories like 'The Story of the Late Mr
Elvesham' by H. G. Wells (108, pp. 406–25). In
the story, a young man, Edward Eden, met an old
man, Egbert Elvesham, who gave him something
rather nasty to drink at a restaurant in Regent
Street. The drink had very peculiar effects. On the
way home Edward Eden had delusions of remembering things that had never happened to him. In
his fuddled state he went to bed, and to sleep. But
sleep did not cure him of his troubles. He (that is,
Edward Eden, according to the story) woke to
find himself in a strange room. 'And then occurred

a thing so trivial and yet so terrible to me that I shiver now to think of that moment. I spoke aloud. I said, "How the devil did I get here?" . . . *And the voice was not my own.*' He told himself he must be dreaming. But he wasn't. Eventually, he got up and lit the candle. 'Then, trembling horribly so that the extinguisher rattled on its spike, I tottered to the glass and saw – Elvesham's face!' He dragged his feeble, heavy limbs to the washhand-stand, and plunged his grey head into a basin of cold water. But it was no good. 'I felt beyond all question that I was indeed Eden, not Elvesham. But Eden in Elvesham's body!'

This, of course, is fictional, but the Identity Question also arises in cases that are claimed to be factual, and said by some people to be cases of 're-incarnation'. Dr Ian Stevenson, in his book *Twenty Cases Suggestive of Reincarnation* (105), describes twenty of the two hundred cases he has personally investigated. Reviewing Stevenson's book, John Beloff writes:

> A typical pattern of events in a good Stevensonian case runs somewhat along the following lines: Somewhere, an individual *A* dies, from some cause or other, perhaps hinting as he does so that in due course he will return to the world. Some years later a small child *B* begins, almost as soon as he has learnt to speak, to talk about people, places and incidents that he insists he remembers from an earlier period when he was 'big'. After much prodding the parents initiate inquiries which

lead to establishing a link between the child *B* and the deceased individual *A*. The climax of the case comes when a confrontation is arranged between the two families. Will *B* recognize *A*'s various relatives and friends? Will he be able to identify *A*'s possessions? The usual effect of being surrounded with *A*'s family and paraphernalia is to produce a fresh crop of memories relating to incidents in *A*'s life. Sometimes *B* feels so strongly this identification with *A* that he will beg to be taken back into *A*'s family. Mostly, however, he learns to adjust to his new circumstances, his obsession with his former life weakens and, by the time he reaches adolescence, even the memories of this former life may have faded entirely. (7)

Unlike the imaginary case of a brain transplant in terms of which I formulated the Identity Question, neither the case of 'The Late Mr Elvesham' nor the so-called 'reincarnation' cases involves something being done to someone's brain. To the best of my knowledge there have not been successful brain transplants. But there have been cases of bisection of the brain, the results of which have been such as might have led the surgeon to ask himself whether he was dealing with one person, or with two people in one body. One case Michael S. Gazzaniga reports in his book *The Bisected Brain* is particularly interesting. As a result of the bisection, and of one brain hemisphere having control over one half of the body, and the other over the other, there was the possibility of antagonistic behaviour between the two halves of the patient's body. The patient, Gazzaniga writes, 'would sometimes find himself pulling down his pants with one hand and pulling them up with the other. Once, he grabbed his wife with his left hand and shook her violently, while with the right trying to come to his wife's aid in bringing the left belligerent hand under control' (34, p. 107).

Whether one describes this, as Gazzaniga does, in terms of *one* person doing one thing with his left hand and something else with his right, or in terms of *two* people in one body, one with a left hand and the other with a right hand, depends on one's answer to the Identity Question. It depends, that is, on what counts as being 'the same person'.

(v) SEEING A LITTLE WAY AHEAD

Now that we have established landmarks, by distinguishing the Unity Question and the Identity Question, it is possible to see a little way ahead. That is, we can see a little of what we need to do in our attempt to rescue Hume from his labyrinth.

It is obvious that to begin with, at any rate, we shall have to take the Unity Question at its face value, and see whether Hume was right to reject the answers to it that he did reject. Do we really have to reject the notion that unity of experiences consists in their all being related to one and the same self-conscious self? Are there not good reasons for accepting this view, reasons Hume never considered? If, after considering these reasons, we are not satisfied, then we must consider the alternatives. Did Hume give the view that experiences are united in all being related to one 'constant and invariable' experience a sufficient hearing? Are there not, in fact, relatively unchanging feelings which provide a background to ones which change from day to day and from minute to minute? If this does not do the trick then we must consider whether Hume's predecessor, John Locke, had not indirectly provided an answer to the Unity Question in what he said about personal identity. He said that a self is the same 'as far as the same consciousness can extend to actions past or to come' (59, Bk II, ch. 27, § 10). This suggests an answer to the Unity Question in terms of 'the extension of consciousness'. But what does Locke mean by 'consciousness' in this connexion?

We must consider all these views, and others that never occurred to Hume, before looking further afield. If none of them satisfy us then we shall have to consider such questions as 'What are the implications of Hume's remark that "self or person is . . . that to which our several impressions and ideas are suppos'd to have a reference"?' and 'To answer the Unity Question do we not first have to answer the Identity Question?'

Looking very far ahead now, I think there is one turn in the labyrinth that I should warn you of before we go any further, lest you should think that my mention of the last question presages an easy solution of the problem. There are philosophers whose investigations into what we should say in answer to questions about personal identity in very bizarre cases have led them to analyse personal identity in terms of 'psychological continuity'. But psychological continuity, presumably, can exist only when there is whatever is meant by talk of the 'unity' of experiences, that is, by experiences being 'in the same mind'. In other words, an experience in one mind cannot be 'psychologically continuous' with one in another. So if these philosophers are right, to answer the Identity Question we have first to answer the Unity Question.

2. ARE WE INTIMATELY CONSCIOUS OF WHAT WE CALL OUR SELF?

One answer to the Unity Question is that the unity of experiences consists in their all being related to one and the same self-conscious self. To this answer Hume would object that 'self or person is not any one impression, but that to which our several impressions are suppos'd to have a reference' (42, p. 251). One philosopher who supposed this was George Berkeley. In this respect Berkeley can be seen as a precursor of Immanuel Kant. Before considering an argument that has been advanced for the self being conscious of itself let us, very briefly, review what Berkeley and Kant said on this question. It is always easier to understand a view on some issue in philosophy if one has first understood other views on the same issue.

(i) BERKELEY'S 'ONE INDIVIDUAL PRINCIPLE'

Berkeley held that the self is known by reflexion, but he meant by this, not that it is introspectible, but that it is known by *thinking*. In other words, the 'reflexion' by which the self is known is the kind of reflexion by which, he says (10, p. 116), we know that the *being* of sensible things is *to be perceived or known*. The self is not known in the way in which the data of sense are known. They are known 'immediately', meaning that we could not fail to know them. The self is known 'immediately' in a different sense; it is known 'intuitively' as opposed to 'demonstratively'; that is, it is known without inference. It is known by the intuition of a necessary connexion of some sort. What sort of necessary connexion? That between ideas (sensations) and their support (spirits). Spirits 'support' ideas in knowing or perceiving them. Without such support ideas could not exist (10, p. 114). The notion of such a support is a relative one. That is, we are acquainted with the other term of the relation, the ideas, only. We know spirits through their relation to those things with which we are acquainted. We know the relation obtains in knowing that it is required by the nature of ideas. We can see how ideas require a spiritual, i.e. a perceiving, support in this way, but we do not perceive the support itself. Material, i.e. non-perceiving, substances could not support ideas in the way required; therefore the notion of them is to be rejected as unintelligible. The substance that supports ideas must be spiritual, i.e. perceiving.

To this it might be objected that what Berkeley calls 'ideas' are really qualities of things – like the softness, moisture, redness and tartness of a cherry, for example; and that the sort of 'support' required by qualities is not that of a perceiver, but that of whatever *has* the qualities, the cherry. Berkeley's reply, in part, would be, I think, that the relation of 'having', whereby the softness, moisture, etc., are united, has not been explained.

In place of this unexplained objective unity he offers us a subjectively determined one:

> Take away the sensations of softness, mois-
> ture, redness, tartness, and you take away the
> *cherry*. Since it is not a being distinct from
> sensations; a *cherry*, I say, is nothing but a
> congeries of sensible impressions, or ideas
> perceived by various senses; which ideas are
> united into one thing (or have one name
> given them) by the mind; because they are
> observed to attend each other. (10, p. 287)

The perceiving spirit is thus not only a support for ideas; it is an agent of unity. 'Ideas are united into one thing by the mind.'

What are the conditions of its being an agent of unity? It would not be such if it were itself a mere collection of ideas. In any case, ideas cannot perceive ideas. It must therefore be 'one individual principle' (10, p. 270), related to its ideas in a one-many relation. There must be a true unity in the perceiver for there to be an attributed unity in the perceived.

(ii) KANT ON THE NECESSARY IDENTITY OF THE SELF AS KNOWER

Like Berkeley's argument, Kant's, in his treatment of the First and Second Paralogisms in the first edition of the *Critique of Pure Reason*, is for a 'subject of thoughts' only – a knower, not something to be known. 'It is obvious that in attaching

"I" to our thoughts we designate the subject of inherence only transcendentally, without noting in it any quality whatsoever – in fact without knowing anything of it either by direct acquaintance or otherwise' (49, A355). Any bringing together of data for knowledge, 'synthesis', requires the identity of that which does the synthesising, but nothing follows, from the existence of this transcendental unity, about a self that could be introspected and found to be identical. 'That I, as a thinking being, persist for myself . . . can by no means be deduced from it' (49, A349).

This is a point that is stressed by commentators on Kant. H. J. Paton explains why there must be a transcendental unity of consciousness in terms of an example. He asks what has to be the case for someone to hear a clock striking twelve *as* a clock striking twelve. He sums up his argument:

> In order to know a series of appearances in time there must be (a) one consciousness, and (b) a concept under which the various appearances are united. It is only when this is so that there is more than a string of subjective sensations, that there is in short an object. The object in this sense is dependent on the unity itself. (75, p. 315)

In the same paper he remarks that 'there can be nothing more misleading than to confuse this question of the necessary identity of the self as knowing with the quite different question of the identity of the self merely as something known (75).

It might be thought that even if one could not infer the identity of the self as something known from the necessary identity of the self as knower, at least one could infer the identity of the 'subject of thoughts'. But Kant seems to want to deny even this. In his treatment of the Third Paralogism he writes that the identity of the transcendental 'I' at different times is

> only a formal condition of my thoughts and their coherence, and in no way proves the numerical identity of my subject. Despite the logical identity of the 'I', such a change may have occurred in it as does not allow of the retention of its identity, and yet we may ascribe to it the same-sounding 'I', which, in every different state, even in one involving change of the subject, might still retain the thought of the preceding subject and so hand it over to the succeeding subject. (49, A363)

He explains this possibility in terms of an analogy. If one elastic ball (such as a billiard ball) hits another in a straight line it communicates its whole state, so far as motion is concerned, to the second. Similarly, we can suppose there to be substances such that one transmits to another all its thoughts. There could be a whole series of such substances, with the ones further down the line, so to speak, accumulating the thoughts of those earlier in the line. 'The last substance would then be conscious of all the states of the previously changed substances, as being its own states, because they would have been transferred to it together with the consciousness of them. And yet it would not have been one and the same person in all these states ' (49, A363 fn.).

For Kant this was a purely empty speculation, to drive home the point that nothing about the identity of a 'subject' could be inferred from the logical identity of the 'I'. But, as we shall see later, it provided William James with a useful model for an answer to the Unity Question.

(iii) AN ARGUMENT FOR THE SELF BEING
        CONSCIOUS OF ITSELF

Now, having seen the strength of the opposition, let us consider an argument that has been advanced for the self being conscious of itself. It is an argument that was advanced by Bertrand Russell, and supported by J. McT. E. McTaggart. In its formulation the terms 'acquaintance' and 'description' are used. Russell explains these terms, and advances the argument, in *The Problems of Philosophy*, chapter 5. The explanation is as follows:

> We shall say that we have *acquaintance* with anything of which we are directly aware, without the intermediary of any process of inference or any knowledge of truths. . . . Thus the sense-data which make up the appearance of my table are things with which I have ac-

quaintance, things immediately known to me just as they are.

My knowledge of the table as a physical object, on the contrary, is not direct knowledge. . . . The table is 'the physical object which causes such-and-such sense-data'. This *describes* the table by means of the sense-data. In order to know anything at all about the table, we must know truths connecting it with things with which we have acquaintance: we must know that 'such-and-such sense-data are caused by a physical object' . . . in such a case we say that our knowledge of the object is knowledge by description. (92, pp. 46–8)

And the argument, for 'thinking that we are acquainted with the "I" ', goes like this:

We know the truth 'I am acquainted with this sense-datum'. It is hard to see how we could know this truth, or even understand what is meant by it, unless we were acquainted with something which we call 'I' . . . Thus, in some sense it would seem we must be acquainted with our selves as opposed to our particular experiences. But the question is difficult, and complicated arguments can be adduced on either side. (92, p. 51)

The two sides for which complicated arguments may be adduced are: (a) the self is something which 'has' or 'owns' particular experiences, and is known by acquaintance, and (b) the self is no more than a collection of particular experiences, related in some way, and is known by description. Russell does not say what the complicated arguments are.

The question is taken up by J. McT. E. McTaggart. McTaggart refers to Russell as having led him to accept the view that the self is known to itself by direct perception. He says that Russell did not work out his position in detail and later ceased to hold it. McTaggart formulates the argument as follows:

> 'I am aware of equality.' This proposition, whether true or false, has certainly a meaning. And, since I know what the proposition means, I must know each constituent of it. I must therefore know 'I'. Whatever is known must be known by acquaintance or by description. If, therefore, 'I' cannot be known by description, it must be known by acquaintance, and I must be aware of it. (64, vol. II, ch. 36, p. 63)

He follows this up with a longish argument intended to prove that 'I' cannot be known by description.

Russell had ceased to hold that the self is known by acquaintance when he wrote *The Analysis of Mind*. His reasoning seems to have been as follows. If I were acquainted with myself I would be conscious of thinking as an act I perform. But I am not. 'Empirically, I cannot discover anything corresponding to the supposed act' (91, pp. 17–18). So I am not acquainted with myself. His revised views are as follows:

> It is supposed that thoughts cannot just come and go, but need a person to think them. Now, of course it is true that thoughts can be collected into bundles, so that one bundle is my thoughts, another is your thoughts, and a third is the thoughts of Mr Jones. But I think the person is not an ingredient in the single thought: he is rather constituted by relations of the thoughts to each other. . . .

> The grammatical forms 'I think', 'you think', and 'Mr Jones thinks', are misleading if regarded as indicating an analysis of a single thought. It would be better to say 'it thinks in me', like 'it rains here' . . . (91, pp. 17–18)

Russell refers to Ernst Mach's *Contributions to the Analysis of Sensations* as 'a book of fundamental importance' in connexion with the view he is expounding. Mach quotes Lichtenberg: 'We know only the existence of our sensations, percepts, and thoughts. We should say, *It thinks*, just as we say, *It lightens*. It is going too far to say, *cogito*, if we translate *cogito* by *I think*' (62).

Russell agrees with Lichtenberg that we should not say 'I think'. But evidently he thinks 'It thinks' is not enough. There must be something to individuate the thinking in question. So he adds 'in me'. But is not saying 'in me' smuggling in 'I' by the back door, so to speak? And so reintroducing a possible object of knowledge by acquaintance? So he adds 'like "it rains here" '. One does not need to know something by acquaintance to use the word 'here' meaningfully. Similarly, he seems to be suggesting, one does not need to know something by acquaintance to use the expression 'in me' meaningfully.

This raises a lot of questions. Let us consider just two of them. (1) Is it true that the word 'here' is an exception to the rule that knowing the meaning of a word means knowing what is meant by it, in the sense of knowing something which we call by that word? (2) Supposing that the word 'here' can be used meaningfully without our knowing something which we call 'here', are Russell and McTaggart right in their assumption that the word 'I' is *not* like 'here' in this respect? In other words, are they right in thinking that a person *must* know something he calls 'I', either by acquaintance or by description, to use the word 'I' meaningfully? (If they are *not* right then we need have no qualms about using the word 'I' in the absence of inward empirical discoveries of thoughts as acts we perform.)

(iv) THE MEANING OF 'HERE'

One use of the word 'here' is the following. My wife, on returning from shopping on Saturday afternoon, calls out 'Where are you?' and I reply 'Here'. She knows, from this, roughly where I am.

But how? Did I *say* where I was? No. She heard
my voice coming from upstairs, or from the
kitchen, or from my workshop. Like most people,
she can tell, just by listening, from what direction
a sound is coming. She learnt, from my saying
'Here', where I was, although I did not *say* where I
was.

I do not *say* where I was and, also, I did not
need to *know* where I was. Suppose that in my
wife's absence I had been knocked unconscious by
a burglar. To give him time to make his getaway he
ties me up, blindfolds me, gags me, and hides me
in a cupboard. I recover consciousness, not
knowing where I am. I manage to bite through the
gag. When I hear my wife I call out 'I'm here', and
she, hearing the sound coming from the cupboard under the stairs, soon releases me. I did not
know where I was, but that did not not stop
me saying 'I'm here'. It would be absurd if my wife
were to accuse me of using the word 'here' without meaning, since I did not know where I was.

But if I did not know where I was, what *did* I
mean by the word? What meaning could it have
had?

Behind this question seems to be the idea that
to talk of the 'meaning' of a word is to talk of some
thing – either some thing in the world (in this case,
a position), which the word stands for, or some
thing in the mind of the person who utters the
word and in the mind of the person who hears it.
(On the latter view, communication is successful
when the things, 'ideas', in the minds of the speaker
and hearer correspond.)

But the idea that to talk of the 'meaning' of a word is to talk of some *thing* does not seem to apply to the use we have been considering of the word 'here'. An utterance like 'Here' can have a *use* without there being something that is *meant* by the word uttered, something which the utterer must know, either by acquaintance or by description, for the utterance to have that use. People know where I am, on hearing me say 'Here', not in virtue of knowing what I mean, but in virtue of being able to locate sounds. 'Cooee' would have served as well.

But is there not a difference between 'Cooee' and 'Here'? Someone who calls out 'Cooee' cannot be said to be saying where he is. But if I say 'Here' in answer to 'Where are you?' am I not saying where I am? After all, if someone with me were to say 'Godfrey is here' surely he would be saying where I was. And if I say 'I'm here' surely I am saying the same thing. So surely I am saying where I am.

There are two distinctions to be borne in mind here, not one.

The first is that between *stating* where someone is and *indicating* where someone is. I shall say that if I say 'I'm in the study' I am stating my whereabouts (though not who 'I' am). But if I say 'I'm here' I am merely indicating my whereabouts. The point is that for the utterance 'I'm here' to serve to inform others of my whereabouts they must be able to locate sounds. They must be able to hear the sounds as coming from some direction. And that they are coming from that direction is not something I say.

The second distinction is that between something having, and not having, a truth-value. Corresponding to this is the distinction between someone being, and not being, right or wrong. Some one who says 'Cooee' is not right or wrong; and what he says is not true or false. But someone who says 'Godfrey is in the study' is right or wrong; what he says is true or false.

We are strongly inclined to think that there is a connexion between these distinctions, a connexion which is expressible as follows. If something is a statement then it is true or false, and the person who makes it is right or wrong. And if something is true or false, and someone who says it is right or wrong, then it is a statement.

With this in mind we argue thus. If someone with me were to say 'Godfrey is here' what he said would be true. He would be right. So he would be stating my whereabouts. But if I say 'I'm here' surely I am saying the same thing. So, equally, I am stating my whereabouts.

But to stop at that would be to ignore another connexion we are inclined to make between the distinctions. This is that if something is *not* something about which I can properly be said to be right or wrong then it is not a statement.

Using this latter connexion we can argue as follows. I can no more be right or wrong in saying 'I'm here' than I can in saying 'Cooee'. So it is not a statement. But if someone with me says 'Godfrey's here' surely he is saying the same as I said. So, equally, he is not making a statement, that is not saying something that is true or false.

Neither of these conclusions is acceptable. In saying 'I'm here' I am indicating, not stating, my whereabouts. And in saying 'Godfrey's here' the person with me is saying something that is true.

If the person with me had said 'Godfrey's in the study' there would have been no doubt about his making a statement. It is because he says 'Godfrey's *here*' that the problem arises. Suppose he had said 'Godfrey's with me'. If others had then asked 'And where are you?' he might have said 'Here'. But to have learnt anything from that they would have had to tell, by listening, from what direction the sound of his voice was coming. That is, he would be indicating, not stating, his own whereabouts. The problem arose because we did not realise that in saying 'Godfrey's here' the person with me was *both* indicating his own whereabouts *and* saying something which was true, namely that I was with him. His *statement* was that I was with him. And when I said 'I'm here' I was *not* saying what he stated.

This could be summed up as follows. I seem to be saying where I am when I say 'I'm here' because I seem to be saying the same thing as someone with me who says 'Godfrey's here'. But all he is *stating* is that I am with him. That he is here is something he is *indicating* by saying 'Godfrey's here', just as I am indicating that I am here when I say 'I'm here'. Only if he said 'Godfrey's in the study' would he be stating where I am without qualification, that is, without it being the case that information was conveyed only in virtue of his indicating something.

Another way of putting this would be to say that when it comes to things that are true or false, people being right or wrong, knowledge and ignorance, it is expressions like 'in the study' that wear the trousers, as J. L. Austin would say. In a language in which expressions had meaning *solely* in virtue of their truth-value there would be no room for the word 'here'.

This is not to say that there cannot be true or false utterances containing 'here'. 'Godfrey's here' is one such. But its being true or false is, in a sense, parasitic on the truth or falsity of utterances not containing 'here', but containing instead expressions like 'in the study'.

There is an interesting corollary to this. We can use expressions like 'in the study' only because we can distinguish one place from another. If we could not distinguish one place from another – which we do by reference to what is at the place, or where it stands in relation to other places – we would have no use for place-names, like 'the study'. But, equally, we would have no use for words like 'here', either in 'Godfrey's here' or in 'I'm here'.

It is tempting to think that I could use 'I'm here' regardless. But it could serve a useful purpose only if I were not a locationless spirit. And if I were not a locationless spirit – that is, if I had a location – then it would not be the case that places could not be distinguished from one another. One place could be distinguished from others, as the place I was in.

(v) THE MEANING OF 'I'

Russell said that rather than say 'I think' it would be better to say 'it thinks in me', like 'it rains here'. Evidently he thought that a person can quite properly use the word 'here' without knowing, either by acquaintance or description, some thing which is what the word means, but that the word 'I' is different, and therefore that someone who cannot, however hard he introspects, discover some thing which is what the word means, should not use it.

But is the word 'I' different? Are there not, in fact, striking resemblances between the uses of 'I' and those of 'here'?

P. T. Geach refers to the Cartesian idea 'that introspection can give the word "I" a special sense, which each of us can learn on his own account'. He reminds us, however, that

> The word 'I', spoken by P. T. G., serves to draw people's attention to P. T. G.; and if it is not at once clear who is speaking, there is a genuine question 'Who said that?' or 'Who is "I"?' Now consider Descartes brooding over his *poêle* and saying: 'I'm getting into an awful muddle – but who then is this "I" who is getting into a muddle?' When 'I'm getting into a muddle' is a soliloquy, 'I' certainly does not serve to direct Descartes's attention to Descartes, or to show that it is Descartes, none other, who is getting into a muddle. We are not to argue, though, that since 'I' does

not refer to the man René Descartes it has some other, more intangible, thing to refer to. Rather, in this context the word 'I' is idle, superflous; it is used only because Descartes is habituated to the use of 'I' in expressing his thoughts and feelings to other people. (35, ch. 26, p. 118)

The use of 'I' in soliloquy may be compared to the use of 'here' in soliloquy. Suppose my wife and I are lost, in cloud, on a mountain. We try to keep in touch by shouting occasionally. 'Where are you?' 'Here'. But we drift apart, and can no longer hear one another. Still lost, I say *to myself*, 'Where am I?' and reply 'Here'. But whereas my wife could have learnt in what direction I was from her had she heard me, there is nothing I can learn from it. It is, as Geach would say, 'idle, superfluous'.

Geach says: 'We are not to argue, though, that since "I" does not refer to the man René Descartes it has some other, more intangible, thing to refer to.' He could have put it more strongly. We are not to argue that 'I' refers to an intangible, invisible, inaudible Cartesian spiritual substance. Can comparison of uses of 'I' with uses of 'here' help us to see why we are not to argue thus?

Instead of uses of 'I' let us consider uses of 'It's me'. (I regard 'It's I' as pedantic.)

Suppose I have lost my memory. All I can find in my pockets is a scrap of paper with a telephone number written on it. Perhaps if I ring the number the person who answers will know who I am. I ring the number, and say 'It's me', hoping for recognition. This case is like the case in which I am lost in cloud and shout out 'Here' to let my wife know where I am. I no more say who I am in this case than I say I am off to my wife's right in the lost-in-cloud case. I do not know, in both cases. And there is an 'idle', soliloquising use of 'It's me' in this case just as there is an 'idle', soliloquising use of 'Here' in the lost-in-cloud case. I am all set to say 'It's me', but nobody answers the phone. Emptily I say to myself: 'It's me, whoever I am.'

Now let us consider my companion's remark 'Godfrey's here'. Is there a use of 'It's me' that is like this? I think there is. Suppose someone asks 'Who is the owner of the new Jaguar XJ12?' and I say 'It's me'. I am saying something that is true or false (false, needless to say).

Finally, is saying 'It's me' in answer to 'Who is the owner, etc.?' of use only because one person can be distinguished from another? I would say so. The questioner must see who answered, or recognise his voice, or something. I am the person whose lips move appropriately when the words 'It's me' are uttered. If everyone's lips moved and everyone spoke with the same accent and intonation then the utterance would be useless. 'It's me' is useful only because 'It's Godfrey' is useful; and 'It's Godfrey' is useful only because I can be identified by features which distinguish me from others.

(vi) TWO SENSES OF 'IDENTITY'?

In order to see how what I have just been saying conflicts with the notion that we are intimately conscious of what we call our self, it is worth turning to the recent writings of H. D. Lewis. It is only with reservations that Lewis can be said to give the answer, to the Unity Question, that the unity of experiences consists in their all being related to the same self-conscious self. His reservations concern not the 'self' part of the answer, but the 'related to' part of it.

'The proper explanation', he writes (57, p. 243), 'comes from one's own inner consciousness of the unique being one finds oneself to be in any experience', but what a person thus finds himself to be is 'not a thing or entity apart from or confronting his experience' (57, p. 233).

What does he mean by the expression 'one's own inner consciousness of the unique being one finds oneself to be in any experience'?

He explains it in terms of a distinction between two senses of 'identity', one of which is 'basic', 'primary', 'fundamental', or 'radical', and the other 'subsidiary or secondary'. 'The consciousness of oneself as a unique and irreducible being' is 'self-identity in its most basic sense' (57, p. 234).

The other sense of identity, the one that he holds to be subsidiary, is the familiar one. For example, I, the Professor of Philosophy at The Open University, am identical with (i.e. am the same person as, i.e. am) the Director of the Royal Institute of Philosophy.

He offers an explanation of how philosophers have gone wrong in their treatment of the problem of self-identity. The explanation is in terms of the two senses of 'identity', his 'basic' sense and the familiar sense, which he calls 'subsidiary or secondary':

> The philosophical discussion of the problem of self-identity has, in my opinion, been much bedevilled by the fact that philosophers have had this sense of their own ultimate indivisible identity at the back of their minds but, not properly grasping just how peculiar and irreducible it is, they have sought, with varying degrees of ingenuity, to account for it in terms of other senses of 'being the same person', such as the ones instanced above. (57, p. 237)

Unfortunately he does not follow this up with illustrations of how, according to him, philosophers have gone wrong. But it is not difficult to construct one.

Lewis holds that memory 'involves the recognition of the past occurrence as one in which I find the consciousness of myself as the person I am now' (57, p. 241). Sydney Shoemaker, on the other hand, has said that 'first-person statements made solely on the basis of memory are not judgments of personal identity at all' (100, p. 124). Presumably Lewis would say that Shoemaker is treating what Lewis calls the 'subsidiary or secondary' sense as if it were the only sense. Shoemaker, he would say, is simply refusing to recognise that there is another sense, which is 'basic' or 'primary', and that memory involves judgements of identity in this other sense.

The question we should be trying to answer is: Are there in fact two senses of 'identity', and is one of them in fact primary and the other secondary?

It would beg the second part of this question to call the two senses, if there are two, 'the primary sense' and 'the secondary sense'. I shall call what Lewis calls 'the primary sense' '*self*-identity', and what Lewis calls 'the secondary sense' '*personal* identity'. (Shoemaker's statement is about *personal* identity.) The question can now be reformulated: Is there self-identity as well as personal identity, and, if so, is self-identity primary and personal identity secondary?

I know my personal identity if I know who I am (the Professor of Philosophy at The Open University, etc.). Suppose (once again) I have lost my memory. I do not know my personal identity. If this happened, then, according to Lewis, it would still be the case that 'I would know myself to be myself' (57, p. 244). I would know my *self*-identity. But what does this mean?

The trouble is that if we attempt to understand this identity by likening it to something else we shall be accused of 'not properly grasping just how peculiar and irreducible it is'. And saying that it is related to personal identity as a primary sense is to a secondary sense would help only if we knew what was meant in this case by saying of two senses that one is primary and the other secondary.

(vii) TWO SENSES OF 'HERE'?

Let us explore further an avenue that was opened up in Section (iv) of this chapter. There are respects in which 'I' functions like 'Here'. Are there two senses of 'Here'?

We distinguished between 'I'm here' said in answer to 'Where are you?' and my companion's remark 'Godfrey's here'.

One difference between the two uses of 'here' can be brought out by considering the difference between saying 'Not here' in answer to 'Where are you?' and in answer to 'Where's Godfrey?' 'Not here' in answer to 'Where's Godfrey?' is straightforwardly true or false. But in answer to 'Where are you?' it is absurd. It has the sort of absurdity that is recognised by authors like A. A. Milne:

> So he bent down, put his head into the hole, and called out:
> 'Is anybody at home?'
> There was a sudden scuffling noise from inside the hole, and then silence.
> 'What I said was, "Is anybody at home?"' called out Pooh very loudly.
> 'No!' said a voice; and then added, 'You needn't shout so loud. I heard you quite well the first time.'
> 'Bother!' said Pooh. (67, p. 22)

In short there is a use of 'here' the denial of which (that is, saying, 'I'm not here') is absurd, and a use the denial of which ('Godfrey's not here') is not

absurd. There is, I shall say, a denial-absurd use
and a denial-not-absurd use.

What would it mean to say that the denial-
absurd sense was primary? It would mean that the
following would make sense.

When I completely lose myself I am no longer
aware of where I am – in one sense, namely that I
do not know where in the world I am. I cannot
place myself as being in London or New York or
Tokyo. But I do, all the same, recognise the place
where I am as the unique place where *I* am. It is
nowhere else. No matter where it may be in the
world I can properly say to myself *'This* is where
I am'. It is only *where* 'this' is that I do not know.
In a more basic sense I have no doubt where I am
– I am *here*, the place I expressly recognise myself to be in in a way which is not possible for
where I am not.

It would also mean, presumably, that we could
not understand the denial-not-absurd sense of
'knowing where I am' unless we first understood
this other sense in which I know where I am even
when I am completely lost. (This would be the
point of calling one sense 'primary' and the other
'secondary'.)

Does Lewis say things about 'I' that are at all
like these things that might be said about 'here'?
He does. He writes:

> When I lose my memory I am no longer aware
> of who I am – in one sense, namely that I do
> not remember my name, where I live, what
> I have been doing in the past and so on. I

cannot place myself in the sense in which the outside observer would place me on the basis of what is known about me. But I do all the same recognize myself as the unique person I am. It is particulars of my past history and situation that I cannot recover. In a more basic sense I have no doubt who I am – I am myself, the being I expressly recognize myself to be in a way which is not possible for knowledge of any other. (57, p. 235)

And with reference to what I have called 'personal identity' he writes: 'I am contending that we cannot give an adequate explanation of this kind of self-identity apart from the peculiar identification of myself as the unique being I am which I have expressly in any experience' (57, p. 243).

H. D. Lewis's book was published in 1969. Prophetically, J. R. Jones said, in 1967, 'The belief dies hard that the nature of consciousness is such as to make it unfailingly self-identifying' (46, p. 1). And, as we shall see in the next chapter, Jones ought to know.

3. THE SELF AS A RELATIVELY CONSTANT MASS OF BODILY FEELING

We began with Hume's 'labyrinth', the state of perplexity into which he got when he asked himself 'whether in pronouncing concerning the identity of a person, we observe some real bond among his perceptions, or only feel one among the ideas we form of them' (42, p. 259). After exploring this labyrinth a little, we established landmarks, in the form of the Unity Question and the Identity Question. The Unity Question is about what unites a succession of experiences, making them the same person's experiences. The Identity Question is about what is essential to personal identity.

Hume's treatment suggests a number of possible answers to the Unity Question. One of them is that the unity of experiences consists in their all being related to one and the same self-conscious self. Hume's reason for denying that the self is conscious of itself is that 'self or person is that to which our several impressions and ideas are suppos'd to have a reference' (42, p. 251). In Chapter 2 we considered an argument for the self being conscious of itself. The argument we considered is Russell's, that to understand 'I am acquainted

with this sense-datum' I must be acquainted with
something I call 'I'. Something Russell says suggests that he would not say that to use the word
'here' in such an utterance as 'It rains here' the
speaker must be acquainted with something he
calls 'here'. Reasons were sought, in features of
our use of expressions like 'I'm here' and 'Godfrey's here', for agreeing with this. A distinction
was drawn between *stating* where someone is
(e.g. 'Godfrey's in the study') and *indicating*
where someone is (e.g. 'I'm here'). 'Here' is used to
indicate where someone is. ('Godfrey's here', said
by someone with me, states where I am – namely
with the speaker – and indicates where the speaker
is.)

Russell thought that his not being able empirically to discover the act of thinking meant that it
would be misleading to say 'I think', that it would
be better to say 'It thinks in me' like 'It rains here'.
But if 'I' is acknowledged to be as much an
indicating word as 'here' is, he need have no such
qualms about using the word 'I'.

I then tried to show that 'I' is like 'here' in the
relevant respects. If the attempt is regarded as
successful then one conclusion to be drawn is that
just as it is utterances containing expressions like
'in the study' that have a truth-value, so it is
utterances containing expressions like 'Godfrey
Vesey' and 'the owner of the Jaguar' that have a
truth-value. They, and not expressions like 'here'
and 'I' wear the trousers, as Austin would say. If
places and people could not be distinguished from
other places and other people then we would have

no indicating use of 'here' and 'I'. But to say this would be to disagree with H. D. Lewis. Lewis distinguishes between two senses of 'identity'. One is the familiar sense, that in which we talk of the police holding identity parades. The other may be called 'self-identity'. Lewis holds that self-identity is primary.

In brief: for the first possible answer to the Unity Question to be acceptable it would have to be the case that people are conscious of their selves; one argument for this is that a person must be acquainted with his self to use the word 'I'; we have found reasons for thinking this argument to be invalid.

Now let us consider the second possible answer.

(ii) J. R. JONES'S THEORY

According to J. R. Jones (48) the unity of the mind consists in experiences being related to another experience which differs from them in being relatively constant.

He develops this answer to the Unity Question in the context of a distinction between what common-sense sentences about selves appear to be about – namely, 'persistent particulars' – and what they are about according to advocates of the 'serial' theory of the self. By the 'serial' theory he means the sort of theory that was held by David Hume, to be examined further in the next chapter. Advocates of this theory declare selves to be complexes of mental events, these mental events being what are ordinarily thought of as the

experiences of selves. On the face of it, advocates
of the serial theory have some explaining to do,
says Jones. 'The first obligation of a theory which
thus declares what is ostensibly a persistent
particular to be a complex of perishing events is
to explain the *unity* of this complex, to explain,
that is, how the events in question are so related
as to appear to constitute an abiding entity' (48,
p. 40).

Jones's own theory is a serial theory modified
to take account of what he calls 'the fact that
individual sensory events seem patently to consist
in the holding of a relation between the sensed
object and something else'. A 'sensory event' is, for
example, my seeing a blue object. He holds that
when I see a blue object there is a relation between
the blue object and 'something else'. This fact, he
says, is neglected by other serialists. They

> tend to take the terms of a self-series, the
> mental events themselves, as unanalysed
> units and to be concerned exclusively with
> naming the relations which bind together
> contemporary events in the unity of the same
> total temporary state and successive total
> temporary states in the unity of the same bio-
> graphy. They give little or no consideration
> to the question of a possible complexity in
> the internal structure of mental events which
> might justify a sceptic in believing that he
> could still patently verify the common owner
> which these relations of co-personalness were
> intended to replace. (48, pp. 41–2)

It is to this question that Jones addresses himself.

He refers, first, to a paper by A. Dorward (25). Dorward, he says, 'shows from an example that, where the internal structure of a *cognitive* event is in question, there is clearly involved a relation between the object cognised and something else which cognises it' (48, p. 42). Jones would agree 'that cognitive events of the kind of which an instance would be my seeing a coloured patch or my hearing a noise, do patently consist in the holding of a relation between something and something else' (48, p. 42). This appears to be in favour of the analysis of the unity of the mind in terms of a persistent particular. A serialist, he remarks, might 'claim that the fact that there appears to be an entity for which I am using "I" as a logically proper name when I say that "*I* am seeing a coloured patch or hearing a noise" is precisely the fact which he thinks is explained' (48, p. 42) by his serialist theory, that is, his answer to the Unity Question. But, writes Jones,

> surely a person never says '*I* am seeing this coloured patch' or '*I* am hearing this noise' *merely* as an expression of the fact that this seeing and this hearing are related to other non-contemporaneous mental events in certain characteristic ways. I at any rate am perfectly certain that there is something *contemporaneous* with my seeing the coloured patch or my hearing the noise to which I mean to relate these objects when I say that it is '*I*'

who am seeing the patch or hearing the noise.
(48, p. 43)

But he does not agree with Dorward that this
'something *contemporaneous*' need be 'a Subject
of awareness, that is, an immaterial persistent
particular whose function it is to perform the
activity of being aware' (48, p. 44).

What is the alternative? It is a paper by Ian Gallie (33) that suggests the answer. People have visual
experiences: things come into, and go out of, their
field of vision. They also have bodily experiences
of various kinds, some short-lived, but others relatively persistent. At any time when something
'comes to light' in their field of vision they will be
aware of their bodily state. The visual field and a
'somatic field' will go hand in hand. When someone says '*I* am seeing a blue object' the 'I' to which
he relates the blue object in saying this, refers to
the somatic field, that is, to his bodily state as he
is aware of it. As Jones puts it, 'The somatic field
in question is the subjective referent to which the
visual datum is related when its occurrence is reported in the sentence "*I* am seeing such and such
a coloured patch" ' (48, p. 60).

Finally, Jones relates his theory to an analysis
of visual perception advanced by C. A. Mace (61,
p. 31). He writes:

> Professor Mace has shown how a purely
> 'visual' percipient, that is, a sentient organism
> equipped with nothing but visual receptors,
> would, for itself, consist merely of an un-

occupied point-of-view. Its visual environment would be presented but, while there would be a place *from which* the environment appeared, there would be nothing *at* that place which might be opposed as 'self' to the surrounding scene. A self cannot consist exclusively of a point-of-view. There must be an experienced occupant of the point-of-view to give rise to self-consciousness. . . . It seems to me, as it does to Mace, that the point-of-view of our imaginary 'visual' percipient becomes occupied in this sense the moment we suppose the data of proprioception to be added to its total sense-field. It then discovers *itself* at its point-of-view. For in its relatively constant mass of bodily feeling, it has now a self to which to refer its outer perceptions. Whereas formerly it could only report its visual experiences (if at all) in statements of the form 'Such and such objects "appear" or "are there" ', it can now report them in the form in which we invariably do report them, namely, by saying that *I* see such and such objects. (48, pp. 60–1)

(iii) CRITICISM OF JONES'S THEORY: DOES THE USE OF 'I' IMPLY 'OWNERSHIP BY A SELF'?

Jones's theory may be criticised at two levels, a superficial level and a deeper level. At the superficial level the question asked would be: Is that to which I relate a coloured patch or a noise when I say 'I am seeing a coloured patch or hearing a noise' really a 'relatively constant mass of bodily feeling'? At the deeper level it would be: When I say 'I am seeing a coloured patch or hearing a noise' am I engaged in relating a coloured patch or a noise to anything?

At the superficial level the sort of objections that might be made to the theory are: (a) If the 'subjective referent' to which a visual datum is related when I say 'I am seeing such and such a coloured patch' is the bodily sensations I am having, what is the 'subjective referent' in the case of my saying 'I am having such and such bodily sensations'? Am I then relating my bodily sensations to themselves? (b) William James (45, vol. 2, p. 456) remarks on having been told by Pierre Janet of an anaesthetic patient – that is, a patient *without* the 'mass of bodily feeling' which is 'the subjective referent' according to Jones's theory – who nevertheless used the word 'I'. Should Janet have told her not to use words without any meaning?

Now let us consider the sort of criticism that might be made at a deeper level.

Jones refers to a view of Samuel Alexander (2, vol. 2, p. 118). Alexander, he writes, 'may be said to have seized on the possibility that mental events may themselves be supposed to "cognise" objects and to have eliminated the reference to their "ownership by a Self" by simply supposing the mind to consist of a collocation of such cognitive events' (48, p. 46). Jones is opposed to this 'no-ownership' view.

Readers who are more familiar with current

philosophical literature than that of fifty years ago
will associate the expression 'no-ownership' not
with Samuel Alexander but with P. F. Strawson.
Strawson (106, pp. 94 ff.) distinguishes two types
of view about the use that we make of the word
'I'. The first type of view is Cartesian. About the
attribution of the second type of view he is more
hesitant. But, he writes, 'there is some evidence
that it was held, at one period, by Wittgenstein
and possibly by Schlick'. He calls the second of
these views the 'no-ownership' or 'no-subject' doctrine of the self.

Let us examine the evidence for attributing this
doctrine to Wittgenstein.

According to G. E. Moore (70, pp. 13–14), to
whom Strawson refers, what Wittgenstein meant
when he said that 'I', in such an utterance as 'I
have tooth-ache', does not denote a possessor, was
that 'the idea of a person doesn't enter into the description of it, just as a [physical] eye doesn't enter
into the description of what is seen'. Wittgenstein
had said something like this in the *Tractatus*
(119, 5.631–5.6331). In the *Philosophische Bemerkungen* (116, p. 94) he says that in pain I can distinguish intensity, localisation, etc., but not the
possessor of pain.

It seems to me to be this same thought that re-
ceives a more 'linguistic' treatment in *The Blue
and Brown Books*. Wittgenstein writes:

> To say 'I have pain' is no more a statement
> *about* a particular person than moaning is.
> 'But surely the word "I" in the mouth of a

man refers to the man who says it; it points to himself; and very often a man who says it actually points to himself with his finger.' But it was quite superfluous to point to himself. He might just as well only have raised his hand. It would be wrong to say that when someone points to the sun with his hand, he is pointing both to the sun and himself because it is *he* who points; on the other hand, he may by pointing attract attention both to the sun and to himself.

The word 'I' does not mean the same as 'L.W.' even if I am L.W., nor does it mean the same as the expression 'the person who is now speaking'. But that doesn't mean: that 'L.W.' and 'I' mean different things. All it means is that these words are different instruments in our language. (118, p. 67)

Following Wittgenstein, we could have said, in the last chapter, that 'in the study' and 'here' are different instruments in our language. In saying 'Here', in answer to 'Where are you?' I am not *referring to* a place as I am if I say 'In the study'.

This point about 'L.W.' and 'I' (and 'in the study' and 'here') being different instruments in our language can be brought to bear on the view of Samuel Alexander to which Jones refers. Alexander's view may be formulated thus: 'The word "I" in "I am seeing a coloured patch" does not refer to a self that owns cognitive events, so perhaps it refers to the cognitive event itself or, rather, to a collocation of such events.' It may then be objected that a mistake has been made in supposing that the word 'I' is the same sort of instrument in our language as a proper name. It may be said that it no more follows from the word 'I' not referring to a self that it refers to something else than it follows from the word 'here' not being the name of a place that it is the name of something else.

This point can equally be brought to bear on Jones's own view, that the word 'I' refers to a relatively constant mass of bodily feeling.

(iv) WILLIAM JAMES'S THEORY: TWO TREATMENTS OF THE QUESTION

William James discusses the Unity Question in the section on 'The Pure Ego' in the chapter of his *Principles of Psychology* entitled 'The Consciousness of Self' (45, vol. 1, pp. 329–42). He treats the matter in two different ways, and the two treatments each take up about half the section. The change from the first treatment to the second occurs at the point (45, vol. 1, p. 336, bottom) where he proposes to turn to 'certain more subtle aspects of the Unity of Consciousness'.

(v) THE FIRST TREATMENT

It is not very obvious what James is getting at in his first treatment of the matter. The following is the crucial passage:

> There is nothing more remarkable in making a judgement of sameness in the first person

than in the second or the third. The intellectual operations seem essentially alike, whether I say 'I am the same' or whether I say 'the pen is the same, as yesterday'. It is as easy to think this as to think the opposite and say 'neither I nor the pen is the same'. . . . The sense of personal identity is . . . the sense of a sameness perceived *by* thought and predicated of things *thought-about*. These things are a present self and a self of yesterday. The thought not only thinks them both, but thinks that they are identical. The psychologist, looking on and playing the critic, might prove the thought wrong, and show there was no real identity . . . the sameness predicated might not obtain, or might be predicated on insufficient grounds. In either case the personal identity would not exist as a *fact*; but it would exist as a *feeling* all the same; the consciousness of it by the thought would be there, and the psychologist would still have to analyse that. (45, vol. 1, pp. 331–2)

What I find puzzling about this is the expression 'no real identity'. It suggests to me that James is concerned, not with *qualitative* sameness (as in 'He wasn't the same after Robert Ford shot him in the back of the head'), but with *numerical* sameness (as in 'He wasn't the man who robbed the bank at Northfield'). If it were not for this expression then, I think, the passage would be reasonably clear. James writes as if a man's earlier and later selves may, or may not, be similar. An emotional shock, or bodily disturbance of some kind, might produce the sort of change which we refer to when we talk of someone being 'a changed man'. He further writes as if such a change might take place without the subject of the change being aware of it – without his thinking that, or feeling as though, any change had taken place. On the other hand, a man's earlier and later selves may, in fact, be similar, and yet, perhaps because of amnesia and his having to learn his biography afresh, and recall the facts of it in a cold abstract way as things he is sure once happened, he would feel, and say, that he was a changed person. The psychologist, however, could tell that there was no real (that is, major) change in him (e.g. in his personality type, temperament, etc.). There would be 'real identity' but nevertheless, to the person concerned, the appearance of a change.

I am fairly sure that this is what James means. If I am right then his first treatment of the unity of the mind is not such as to provide an answer to the Unity Question.

(vi) THE SECOND TREATMENT

The inspiration for James's second treatment seems to have been Kant's speculation as to how there might be the appearance of identity in a subject, without real identity. We considered that in Chapter 2, Section (ii). James writes:

> As Kant says, it is as if elastic balls were to have not only motion but knowledge of it,

and a first ball were to transmit both its motion and its consciousness to a second, which took both up into *its* consciousness and passed them to a third, until the last ball held all that the other balls had held, and realized it as its own. It is this trick which the nascent thought has of immediately taking up the expiring thought and 'adopting' it, which is the foundation of the appropriation of most of the remoter constituents of the self. Who owns the last self owns the self before the last, for what possesses the possessor possesses the possessed. It is impossible to discover any *verifiable* feature in personal identity, which this sketch does not contain. (45, vol. 1, pp. 339–40)

On this theory, two experiences, an earlier one and a later one, are in the same mind if the 'thought' that possesses the later experience has 'adopted' the thought that possessed the earlier one, or if there has been a succession of such adoptions linking the two experiences.

James realises that there are limits to the 'adoption' analogy. In the literal use of the term 'adopt', a person adopts someone else's child. Two different people, in succession, have the child. In James's theory, who, or what, has the experiences? James calls it 'the nascent thought'. He evidently sets store on features named in a theory being 'verifiable'. Is the existence of the nascent thought verifiable? James's answer is a qualified one. 'It may feel its own immediate existence – we have all along admitted the possibility of this, hard as it is by direct introspection to ascertain the fact – but nothing can be known *about* it till it is dead and gone.'

What does James mean by talk of our *feeling* the existence of the thought?

The answer is given earlier on in the chapter (45, vol. 1, pp. 296–302), where James is trying to describe what it is, in our subjective life as a whole, our whole 'stream of thought', which we identify as our innermost self. It is that about which he says: 'Compared with this element of the stream, the other parts, even of the subjective life, seem transient external possessions, of which each in turn can be disowned, whilst that which disowns them remains'. He remarks that when people try to define the nature of this innermost self opinions begin to diverge. 'Some would say that it is a single active substance, the soul, of which they are thus conscious; others, that it is nothing but a fiction, the imaginary being denoted by the pronoun I.' About its nature he himself is in no doubt. 'This central part of the Self is *felt*.'

This leads on to the question, 'Now can we tell more precisely in what the feeling of this central active self consists?'

James's first general description of the feeling is in terms of 'a constant play of furtherances and hindrances' in his thinking, 'of checks and releases, tendencies which run with desire, and tendencies which run the other way'. But he is dissatisfied with this general description. He wants to come to 'the closest possible quarters with the facts'. When he does so, he writes,

> it is difficult for me to detect in the activity any purely spiritual element at all. Whenever my introspective glance succeeds in turning round quickly enough to catch one of these manifestations of spontaneity in the act, all it can ever feel distinctly is some bodily process, for the most part taking place within the head. (45, vol. 1, p. 300)

The implications of this for the Unity Question are that it is these feelings of bodily processes, mostly in the head, to which are appropriated 'expiring thoughts': '*These are the real nucleus of our personal identity. . . .* They are the kernel to which the *represented* parts of the Self are assimilated, accreted, and knit on' (45, vol 1, p. 341).

The upshot is that James's adoption theory seems not to differ significantly from J. R. Jones's theory to the effect that the unity of the mind consists in experiences being related to a 'relatively constant mass of bodily feeling'. What difference there is consists in (a) the use by James of the metaphor of 'adoption' or 'appropriation' – the main point of which seems to be a negative one; namely, that 'consciousness of personal identity . . . can be fully described without supposing any other agent than a succession of perishing thoughts', and (b) the assertion by Jones that the mass of bodily feeling in question is 'relatively constant'.

This being so, James's theory will be open to the sort of objections to which Jones's theory is open. But there are also more obvious objections, those given by A. J. Ayer in his discussion of James's theory in *The Origins of Pragmatism* (5, pp. 268–70).

(vii) AYER'S OBJECTIONS TO JAMES'S THEORY

Ayer objects, to James's theory, that it leads to counter-intuitive results. That is, its effect is to deny unity of mind where common sense does not deny it, and to assert it where common sense does not assert it. He cites three cases. (a) The adopting, or appropriating, process would be interfered with if someone were to have a lapse of consciousness followed by loss of memory. Yet we would not ordinarily deny that his earlier and later experiences were the same person's experiences. (b) People may have dreams 'which are completely self-contained, in the sense that they neither include any thoughts which appropriate previous experiences nor have any constituents which are appropriated by subsequent thoughts'. On James's theory we should have to deny that such dream-experiences occur in the same mind as waking-experiences. (c) On the other hand, Ayer says, 'there is no contradiction in supposing that I sometimes fall into the error of "reviving" experiences which either did not occur at all or occurred in situations at which I was not physically present'. I am dubious about this last case. Ayer writes: 'If I appropriate an experience which was attached to a different body from the one to which my present experiences belong, it will normally follow that I am appropriating the experiences of another person'. If 'it will normally follow that . . .' means 'people would ordinarily say that . . .', then I think that the situation envisaged (people appropriating experiences attached to other people's bodies) is so strange that most people would not know what to say. Perhaps they would say that they could not understand what was meant by 'appropriating' in this context. But if so, then this, in itself, has a bearing on James's theory. If it is not *meaningful* to talk of appropriating other people's experiences then 'A past experience having been mine consists in my appropriating it' begins to look suspiciously like a proposition that is tautologous because of a restriction on the application of 'appropriated'.

4. UNITY CONSTITUTED BY RELATIONS AMONG EXPERIENCES

(i) LOCKE AND 'THE IDENTITY OF CONSCIOUSNESS'

We began with Hume's 'labyrinth', and established landmarks in the form of the Unity Question and the Identity Question. Hume's treatment suggests a number of possible answers to the Unity Question. We have, so far, considered two of them. The first was that fleeting experiences are united in being related to a self-conscious self. The second was that they are united in being related to an enduring experience. We did not find either of these answers to be satisfactory. The third answer suggested by Hume's treatment is that fleeting experiences are united in being related *to one another* in some way. Hume holds that there are three ways in which experiences may be related: contiguity, resemblance and causation. The first of these, contiguity, 'has little or no influence in the present case', he says (42, p. 260). Resemblance could arise from some experiences being memories of others, since memory is 'a faculty, by which we raise up the images of past perceptions' and such images necessarily resemble their objects (42, pp. 260–1). But Hume sees an objection. It may be a sufficient condition but it can hardly be a necessary one – simply because experiences get forgotten. If an experience is entirely forgotten then there is no present experience to resemble it in being a memory of it. So if we were to treat resemblance based on memory as the relation which unites experiences we could not admit that an entirely forgotten experience and a present experience could be experiences of the same person.

This seems so obvious that it is hard to believe that anyone could have thought otherwise. Did John Locke think otherwise?

Locke, like Hume, did not distinguish between the Unity Question and the Identity Question. He did, however, distinguish between questions about the identity of soul, person, and man. What he said about personal identity *might* be interpreted as an answer to the Unity Question in terms, not of resemblance resulting from some experiences being memories of others, but of memory itself. I say 'might' because it is so difficult to pin Locke down. He says that 'personal identity consists . . . in the identity of consciousness' (59, Bk II, ch. 27, § 19). By 'consciousness' he means something that can be 'interrupted by forgetfulness' (59, Bk II, ch. 27, § 10). On the other hand he allows for the possibility of a person extending his consciousness back to actions done by people long since dead and buried. What Locke would say, under these circumstances, is that the person who extends his consciousness back 'finds himself the same person' as the person who performed the actions. (§ 14: 'Let him once find himself conscious of any of the actions of Nestor, he then finds himself the same person with Nestor.')

One can take this in two ways. Either Locke does mean 'remembers' by 'extends his consciousness back' and, accepting the inference that if *X* remembers doing what *Y* did then *Y* is the same person as *X*, draws the paradoxical conclusion that I can be the same person as someone long since dead and buried. Or he means 'seems to remember' by 'extends his consciousness back'. Which does he mean?

It would be wrong for God, at the Day of Judgement, to punish me for the actions of Nestor if I merely *seem* to remember performing them. But, Locke says (in § 26), 'at the great day . . . the sentence shall be justified by the consciousness all persons shall have that they themselves, in what bodies soever they appear, or what substances soever that consciousness adheres to, are the same that committed those actions, and deserved that punishment for them'. In other words if I think, rightly (being Nestor), or wrongly (not being Nestor), that I did what Nestor did then I am to be punished for Nestor's deeds. *If* Locke means 'seems to remember' by 'extends his consciousness back', and *if* he is not prepared to endorse people being punished for what they have not done, then he must somehow rule out the possibility of people seeming to remember doing things they did not do. Conversely, if he is concerned to rule out this possibility then that suggests that he *does* mean 'seems to remember' by 'extends his consciousness back'.

In § 13 he writes:

Why one intellectual substance may not have represented to it as done by itself what it never

did, and was perhaps done by some other
agent . . . will be difficult to conclude from
the nature of things. And that it never is so,
will by us, till we have clearer views of the
nature of thinking substances be best resolved
into the goodness of God, who . . . will not by
a fatal error of his creatures transfer from one
to another that consciousness which draws re-
ward or punishment with it.

In other words, Locke *is* concerned to rule out the
possibility that people, at the Day of Judgement,
will seem to remember doing, and so be punished
for doing, things they did not do. God, in his
mercy, will not allow it to happen.

I conclude, though rather hesitantly, that Locke
means 'seems to remember' by 'extends his consciousness back'. I am hesitant about this conclusion because it leaves Locke in the unenviable
position of holding both (a) that 'personal identity
consists . . . *in* the identity of consciousness' (§ 19,
my italics), and (b) that consciousness of having
performed some action is theoretically, even if not
actually (because God fixes things so that it does
not happen), compatible with its being someone
else who did it (the apparent implication of what
Locke says in §§ 13 and 26). And this looks very
much like inconsistency.

But if, on the other hand, Locke means 'remembers' by 'extends his consciousness back' then
there is another objection to which he is open. It
is that just as '*p* is true' is a condition of 'I know
p' being true so 'I am *X*' is a condition of 'I remem-

ber doing what only X did' being true. Trying to
analyse personal identity in terms of memory is
like trying to analyse truth in terms of knowledge. As Butler said, 'One should really think it
self-evident, that consciousness of personal identity
presupposes, and therefore cannot constitute,
personal identity; any more than knowledge, in any
other case, can constitute truth, which it presupposes' (14, § 3).

Another classic objection to Locke's account of
personal identity is that advanced by Thomas
Reid. He argues that it is a consequence of Locke's
doctrine that a man may be, and at the same time
not be, the person who did a particular action:

> Suppose a brave officer to have been flogged
> when a boy at school, for robbing an orchard,
> to have taken a standard from the enemy in
> his first campaign, and to have been made a
> general in advanced life: suppose also, which
> must be admitted to be possible, that, when
> he took the standard, he was conscious of his
> having been flogged at school, and that when
> made a general he was conscious of his tak-
> ing the standard, but had absolutely lost the
> consciousness of his flogging. These things be-
> ing supposed, it follows from Mr Locke's
> doctrine, that he who was flogged at school
> is the same person who took the standard, and
> that he who took the standard is the same
> person who was made a general. Whence it
> follows, if there be any truth in logic, that the
> general is the same person with him who was

flogged at school. But the general's consciousness does not reach so far back as his
flogging – therefore, according to Mr Locke's
doctrine, he is not the person who was
flogged. Therefore the general is, and at the
same time is not, the same person with him
who was flogged at school. (88, pp. 213–14)

(ii) HUME AND 'THAT CHAIN OF CAUSES AND
    EFFECTS WHICH CONSTITUTE OUR SELF OR
    PERSON'

Having dismissed contiguity of experiences as irrelevant, and having seen good reason to reject
resemblance due to memory as the unity-provid-
ing relation among experiences, Hume was left
with the relation of causation. 'The true idea of the
human mind, is to consider it as a system of
different perceptions or different existences, which
are link'd together by the relation of cause and
effect, and mutually produce, destroy, influence,
and modify each other' (42, p. 261). 'Memory does
not so much *produce* as *discover* personal identity,
by showing us the relation of cause and effect
among our different perceptions' (42, p. 262).

What was his objection to this account? Why
did he say that 'nothing but the seeming evidence
of the precedent reasonings cou'd have induc'd me
to receive it?' (42, p. 635).

Hume does not say, but it is not difficult to
guess. He realised that since causal relations among
experiences 'may diminish by insensible degrees,
we have no just standard, by which we can decide

any dispute concerning the time, when they acquire or lose a title to the name of identity' (42, p. 262). I think he wanted a just standard. And I think that he knew, when he laid aside his philosophy, that we *have* a standard other than the one to which his 'precedent reasonings' led him.

5. WHY NOT THE OBVIOUS ANSWER TO THE UNITY QUESTION?

(i) THE OBVIOUS ANSWER

We have now considered all the answers to the Unity Question suggested by Hume's treatment. The first was that fleeting experiences are united in one mind in being related to one and the same self-conscious self (Chapter 2). The second was that they are united in being related to an enduring experience (Chapter 3). The third was that they are united in being related to one another in some way (Chapter 4). We have seen that there are objections, either obvious or not so obvious, to all of them.

And yet has not the answer been staring us in the face all the time? *Two experiences are the same person's experiences if they are experiences had by the same person.* Is it not obvious (a) that the Unity Question is answered by answering the Identity Question, that is, by saying what we mean by 'the same person', and (b) that, people being creatures of flesh and blood, there is no problem about saying what we mean by 'the same person'?

Would that it were that simple! In philosophy nothing is obvious to everyone. Specifically, it is not obvious to A. J. Ayer that the Unity Question is answered by answering the Identity Question. And it is not obvious to René Descartes that we are creatures of flesh and blood. And it is not obvious to a very great number of philosophers writing in the last twenty years or so that there is no problem about saying what we mean by 'the same person'. Indeed, to some philosophers, not necessarily for Cartesian reasons, it has seemed that the Identity Question can be answered only by first answering the Unity Question. So we are not yet out of the wood or, rather, Hume's labyrinth.

In this chapter let us consider the reasons of Descartes and Ayer for not giving what I called, in the chapter title, 'the obvious answer'. The remainder of the book can then be devoted to the question of 'the criteria of personal identity'.

(ii) WHY NOT: DESCARTES

Descartes knew how we ordinarily think of ourselves, namely as flesh and blood people, that is, in Strawson's words, as 'a type of entity such that *both* predicates ascribing states of consciousness *and* predicates ascribing corporeal characteristics, a physical situation, etc., are equally applicable' (106, p. 102). In a letter to Princess Elizabeth of Bohemia, dated 28 June 1643, Descartes wrote:

> I supposed that your Highness still had very much in mind the arguments proving the distinction of soul and body; and I did not wish to ask you to lay them aside, in order to represent to yourself that notion of their union which everybody always has in himself without doing philosophy – viz. that there is one single person who has at once body and consciousness, so that this consciousness can

move the body and be aware of the events
that happen to it. (24, p. 281)

The 'arguments proving the distinction of soul
and body' were ones he had advanced in Part IV
of the *Discourse on the Method* and in the Second
and Sixth of the *Meditations on First Philosophy*
(24, pp. 31–2, 66–71, 114–15).

The argument in the *Meditations* goes something like this. For me to think at all I must exist.
Therefore 'I exist', when I think it, cannot but be
true. Therefore I cannot think 'I exist', and doubt
its truth. Therefore I have only to think 'I exist'
to be certain of its truth. Therefore inasmuch as
I can think 'I exist' I am certain that I exist. But at
the same time as being certain that I exist I can
(because I might be dreaming, be deceived by an
extremely powerful malicious demon, etc.) doubt
that I have a body. Therefore in so far as I am certain of my existence I am no more than a thinking
being. Therefore I can think of myself existing as
simply a thinking being, that is, as a being distinct
from a body. But God, being omnipotent, could
have made me as I can think of myself, and if God
could have made me as a being distinct from a body,
then I really am distinct from a body.

Descartes's argument has been subjected to
a great deal of criticism ever since it was first pro-
pounded. Descartes's friend, the Rev. Father Mer-
senne, circulated the *Meditations* among various
philosophers and theologians. Their criticisms
were forwarded to Descartes, who in turn commented on them, and published the whole discus-

sion, along with the *Meditations*. There is not the space in this book to do more than give one example of the sort of criticisms that were advanced.

The Jansenist theologian and philosopher, Antoine Arnauld, in the 'Fourth Set of Objections urged against the Meditations' (23, vol. 2, p. 83), argued that on Descartes's principles of reasoning it should be possible for there to be a right-angled triangle without properties every right-angled triangle must have, and therefore that the principles must be wrong. The argument goes like this. A person can be certain that 'the angle in a semi-circle is a right angle and that hence the triangle made by this angle and the diameter is right-angled' and, at the same time, doubt that 'the square on its base is equal to the squares on the sides of the right-angled triangle' – simply because he is not very good at geometry. He can, therefore, think of the triangle as being right-angled *and* as not being such that the square on the hypotenuse equals the sum of the squares on the other two sides. According to Descartes, God, being omnipotent, could have made a triangle like this, thus proving that it is not essential to a right-angled triangle that the square on its hypotenuse should equal the sum of the squares on the other two sides. But we can see that it *is* essential, and therefore the reasoning must be invalid. So it does not follow from the possibility of my thinking of myself as a thinking being at the same time as doubting that I have a body that I am distinct from my body.

iii) THE INFLUENCE OF DESCARTES

To say that a person is distinct from his body is to say that questions about the identity of a person are questions about something that is not essentially bodily. And to say this is positively to invite answers to questions about personal identity in terms of an 'I', 'self', 'mind', 'consciousness', or whatever. That 'most philósophers seem inclin'd to think that personal identity *arises* from consciousness' (Hume, quoted in Chapter 1) is a direct result of the influence of Descartes.

We can now understand another feature of a good many of the answers to the Unity Question that we have been considering. In most cases no distinction is drawn between an answer to the Unity Question and one to the Identity Question. The explanation is that if the Identity Question is a question about the identity of something that is not essentially bodily then an answer to the Unity Question, if one could only be found, would be, at the same time, an answer to the Identity Question. Or, rather, there is only one question: How are 'the whole train of perceptions . . . *united by identity*' (42, p. 259, my italics)?

(iv) WHY NOT: AYER

Ayer is primarily concerned with the question 'In what does a person's ownership of states of consciousness consist?'

It is almost as if he had read the passage from Wittgenstein's *Blue and Brown Books* quoted in

Chapter 3, agreed with the view Wittgenstein rejects ('Surely the word "I" in the mouth of a man refers to the man who says it'), and looked to the answer to the Identity Question for an account of 'the man' and to J. S. Mill (66, ch. 12) for an account of how states of consciousness are related to 'the man'.

Mill, if he were purged of his phenomenalism, would say, in answer to the Unity Question, that two sensations are the same person's sensations if they are connected with the same body (that person's body). The required manner of 'connexion' is that the body is present as an antecedent condition of the sensations, and must change in some way for the person whose body it is to have them. In other words, I cannot have sensations of the paper on which I am writing without having sense-organs and a brain, and without the paper producing changes in those sense-organs and brain.

Ayer is 'inclined to think that a person's ownership of states of consciousness consists in their standing in a special causal relation to the body by which he is identified' (4, p. 116). His problem is to say what this 'special causal relation' is. It must be such that 'any individual experience is limited to one and only one human body' (4, p. 118). It cannot be simply the relation of causal necessity, for 'every one of my experiences is dependent upon the existence of bodies other than my own. This follows simply from the fact that I must have had ancestors' (4, p. 119).

He meets this difficulty by distinguishing between 'mediate' and 'immediate' causal necessity. His ancestors' bodies are only mediately necessary for the occurrence of his experiences. Consideration of certain para-normal cases leads him to refine this further. Only the 'internal states' of bodies are to be regarded as relevant. Then, 'certain experiences would be mine in virtue of the fact that such things as the condition of my brain and nerves were immediately necessary for their occurrence, and that they did not stand in precisely this relation to any other body but my own' (4, p. 123).

Ayer's answer to the Unity Question, and his whole treatment of the problem, is particularly interesting in that, unlike some of the other philosophers whose answers to the Unity Question we have been considering, he has seen the difference between the Unity Question and the Identity Question. Moreover, when he gives his answer to the Unity Question it is with the appearance of being justified in giving it by his answer to the Identity Question:

> I think, therefore, that the most that we can hope to maintain is that an experience belongs to a given person in virtue of the fact that some state of that person's body is a necessary condition of its occurrence. The justification for this would be first that experiences are individuated only by reference to the persons who have them, and secondly that persons are identified only by reference to their bodies. (4, p. 119)

What are we to make of Ayer's answer (and Mill's, in so far as it is the same as Ayer's)?

Probably with Mill in mind, McTaggart discussed the theory that two mental states 'belong to the same self when, and only when, the same living body (or what appears as such) stands in a certain relation of causality to both of them' in *The Nature of Existence*. He noted that according to the theory all that makes mental states part of the same self is the *indirect* relation through the body, and commented:

> But if there is no relation but the indirect relation, then no man has any reason to say that any two states belong to the same self unless he has a reason to believe them to be caused by the same body. And this means that the vast majority of such statements as 'I was envious yesterday' are absolutely untrustworthy. In the first place, by far the greater number of them have been made by people who have never heard of the doctrine that emotions and judgments are caused by bodily states. . . . In the second place, even those people who have heard of the doctrine that all mental states are caused by bodily states and who accept it, do not, in far the greater number of cases, base their judgments that two states belong to the same self on a previous conviction that they are caused by the same body. . . . Thus this theory would involve that every judgment of the type 'I am *x*', or 'I was *x*', or 'I did *x*', . . . is totally un-

trustworthy. Such scepticism, even if not absolutely self-contradictory, which I think it is, is so extreme that it may be regarded as a *reductio ad absurdum*. (64, vol. 2, ch. 36, pp. 73–4)

Ayer has a reply to this. He says that in saying 'that a person's ownership of states of consciousness consists in their standing in a special causal relation to the body by which he is identified', he is 'not maintaining, of course, that this is how one actually becomes aware of one's own experiences, but only that the fact that they are one's own, or rather the fact that they are the experiences of the person that one is, depends upon their being connected with this particular body.'

Whether this is all right or not depends on what is meant by 'a causal relation'. Elsewhere Ayer explains what he means by talk of a causal relation between mental and physical events:

> The facts are that the physiologist makes certain observations, and that these observations fall into different categories. On the one hand there are the observations which lead him to tell his story about nerve cells and electrical impulses. That is to say, the story is an interpretation of the observations in question. On the other hand there are the observations which he interprets by saying that the subject of his experiment is in such and such a 'mental' state, that he is thinking, or resolving to perform some action, or feeling some

sensation, or whatever it may be. . . . It seems
to me that when it is asserted that the two
events in question – the mental and the
physical – are causally connected . . . all that
is meant, or at least all that can be properly
meant, is that these two sets of observations
are correlated in the way that I have
described. (54, pp. 71–2)

There is no problem about the interpretation of
observations in terms of nerve cells and electrical
impulses. But what about the interpretation of
other observations in terms of mental states? The
subject moans, and the physiologist says 'He's in
pain'. Does he say this because he has, in the past,
correlated other people's moans with other
people's feelings of pain? But how could he have
observed other people's feelings of pain except by
treating X's moans as expressing X's pain? In
short, does not the second interpretation involve
acceptance of a non-causal criterion of ownership
of states of consciousness?

Ayer seems to be aware of the objection that for
it to be meaningful to talk of a causal relation between experiences and bodies, experiences must be
identifiable independently of bodies. He asks:
'How could we ever have set about discovering
[psycho-physical laws] unless the experiences,
which were found to be correlated with certain
physical states, had themselves been independently
identified?' (4, p. 125).

His reply to this objection consists in drawing
'a distinction between the general proposition that

every experience is causally dependent, in the required sense, upon a body, and the more specific propositions which describe the different forms that this dependence takes' (4, p. 125). The former he holds to be a necessary proposition 'on the ground that causal dependence upon a body is an essential part of what we mean by an experience' (4, pp. 125–6). The latter are contingent.

The latter, I presume, are such propositions as that experiences of an emotional type are causally connected with changes in the hypothalamus. About them, Ayer says: 'The precise nature of the psycho-physical laws which correlate experiences of various types with certain sorts of physical conditions remains a matter for empirical discovery' (4, p. 126).

It is not clear how drawing this distinction enables Ayer to meet the charge of circularity. What he has to show is that our identifying X's experiences as we do is not incompatible with there being a causal (i.e. an empirically discoverable) relationship between X's experiences in general and X's body in general. That the relationship of 'experiences of various types with certain sorts of physical conditions' is empirically discoverable, is beside the point. Such discovery presupposes our regarding what X says and does as expressing X's experiences.

Leaving aside, then, the 'specific propositions', we are left with the assertion that the 'proposition that every experience is causally dependent, in the required sense, upon a body . . . must be held to be necessary, on the ground that causal dependence upon a body is an essential part of what we mean by an experience' (4, pp. 125–6).

But what are Ayer's grounds for holding 'that causal dependence upon a body is an essential part of what we mean by an experience'?

In discussing Physicalism, earlier, he had said that

> it does not follow [from statements about experiences not being equivalent to statements about bodies] that it is even logically possible for states of consciousness to exist independently of any physical body. The reason why it does not follow is that it may not make sense to talk of states of consciousness except as the experiences of some conscious subject; and that it may well be that this conscious subject can not be identified except by reference to his body. (4, p. 113)

Let us grant that an experience can be identified only by reference to a conscious subject, and that a conscious subject can be identified only by reference to his body. Does it follow 'that causal dependence upon a body is an essential part of what we mean by an experience'? Surely not, if, as Ayer holds, (a) to assert two things (in this case, an experience and a state of the body of a conscious subject) to be causally connected is to assert two sets of observations to be correlated in a certain way, and (b) the experiences that are the subject-matter of one of the two sets of observations cannot be identified independently of the conscious subjects, states of the bodies of whom are the subject-matter of the other of the two sets of observations.

The problem is not that of correlating, say, tears on the one hand and states of the brain of the person who is crying on the other. It is that of correlating feelings of pain on the one hand and tears on the other. To ask 'Whose feeling of pain do the tears that are streaming down Jones's cheeks express?' is to exhibit a lack of comprehension of the logic of the language of experience. We shall examine this logic in Chapter 8.

6. ARE PERSONS IDENTIFIED ONLY BY REFERENCE TO THEIR BODIES?

(i) REVIEW

The 'obvious' answer to the Unity Question is that two experiences are the same person's experiences if they are experiences had by the same person. In the last chapter I asked whether it is not obvious (a) that the Unity Question is answered by answering the Identity Question, that is, by saying what we mean by 'the same person', and (b) that, people being creatures of flesh and blood, there is no problem about saying what we mean by 'the same person'. We considered, very briefly, Descartes's argument for our not being creatures of flesh and blood (or, rather, not *essentially* such creatures); and, at greater length, Ayer's view that an answer to the Identity Question still leaves the way open for an answer, in terms of experiences being causally related to events in a brain, to the Unity Question. The discussion of Ayer's view made evident the need for greater clarity about the logic of the language of experience. And to this we shall have to return. But, first, let us take up Ayer's remark that 'persons are identified only by reference to their bodies' (4, p. 119). Is he right?

(ii) SELF-IDENTIFICATION

Suppose I have been in an accident, and when I recover consciousness cannot remember even who

I am. But gradually things come back to me, and I remember what my name is, where I live, what I do for a living, and so on. I 'identify' myself – but without reference to a body. (I do not have to observe the words 'I can remember who I am now' coming out of a certain mouth, to remember who I am.)

The possibility of my identifying someone, namely myself, other than by observing something about someone, might be thought to raise the question whether *I* could know myself to be so-and-so although *others*, relying on what was observable, would have said I was someone else. Is it at least theoretically possible that I should be Godfrey Vesey although to all appearances I am Charlie Monk?

I should not have said 'to *all* appearances'. I now have Charlie Monk's body. But out of the mouth of that body come the protesting words 'But I'm not Charlie Monk. I'm Godfrey Vesey'.

Is this theoretically possible? And, if so, is it something that could happen quite often? Or could it only happen as an exception to the rule – the rule being that personal identity and bodily identity go hand in hand?

Perhaps we should begin at the beginning, and ask: Must personal identity and bodily identity as a rule go hand in hand?

There are two arguments for an affirmative answer to this question. One concerns how people are individuated. The other concerns memory.

In saying '*This person* is in fact Jack Jones, in spite of looking just like Charlie Monk' we individuate the person about whom we are talking as 'this person'. Our hearer takes us to mean the person before us. If he did not do so he would not know who was the subject of our remarks. And 'Jack Jones' and 'Charlie Monk' are names, and names get the sort of meaning they have in virtue of some name-giving performance. But this performance requires that Jack Jones and Charlie Monk should be distinguishable from other people, and from one another. And how can we distinguish between people except by reference to what is observable of them – their bodies? It is no accident that 'someone' and 'somebody' are synonyms. If the personal names 'Charlie Monk' and 'Jack Jones' could not be brought into our language, in the first place, by naming (corporeal) people, then I cannot see how such a statement as 'The person who looks just like Charlie Monk is in fact Jack Jones' could have any use. It is a case of the exception proving the rule. In understanding the exception we presuppose the rule.

The argument concerning memory takes its departure from the fact that it can seem to people that they are remembering doing things they have not in fact done. A person may very much have wanted to do a certain thing, and have vividly imagined himself doing it. But someone else may in fact have done it. At the time the person knows he has not done what he wanted to do. But he forgets, and later mistakes his memory of what he imagined doing for a memory of what he did. It then seems to him that he is remembering doing what was in fact done by someone else.

A good example of this is the case of the shell-shocked brother in Dorothy L. Sayers's novel, *The Unpleasantness at the Bellona Club*. He sincerely confessed to a murder he had not committed.

Now, for the person before us really to be the person who committed the murder, he must not merely *seem* to remember doing it; he must *really* remember doing it. So for us to use memory-claims to establish personal identity we need some means of distinguishing real from seeming memories. But surely, to answer the question 'Does he really remember committing the murder?' we have to answer the question 'Did he, and not somebody else, do it?' In other words, we distinguish between real, and seeming, memories in terms of who, in fact, did what somebody claims to remember having done. Unless we have some means of establishing who did something, which is independent of the memory-claims people make, we cannot use their memory-claims as a means. For us to mean anything by 'memory', real memory must, *in principle*, be distinguishable from seeming memory. And the distinction cannot itself be in terms of memory.

If the person who claimed to remember committing the murder has not the same body as the person who did commit it, then we would, *ordinarily*, say that he merely seemed to remember doing it. That is, we would not ordinarily treat the memory-claim as establishing the identity of the person before us with the murderer in the face of the evidence that it was some*body* else who did it.

I have used words like 'in principle' and 'ordinarily' here to indicate that I can see no reason in the condition of our having the concept of memory (namely, that as a rule personal identity and bodily identity go hand in hand) for excluding the theoretical possibility of an exception to the rule.

But it has been argued, notably by Bernard Williams, that an exception is not even theoretically possible.

(iii) BERNARD WILLIAMS'S QUESTION

Bernard Williams begins the third paragraph of a paper entitled 'Personal Identity and Individuation' (113) with the words: 'I shall try to show that bodily identity is always a necessary condition of personal identity' (113, p. 230). Evidently he is trying to show not merely that *as a rule* personal identity and bodily identity go hand in hand, but that the rule cannot have exceptions. His argument hinges on an imaginary case in which two people, Charles and Robert, make memory-claims that fit the pattern of Guy Fawkes's life. For instance they both claim to remember doing the things Guy Fawkes did. About this, Williams writes:

> They cannot both be Guy Fawkes; if they were, Guy Fawkes would be in two places at once, which is absurd. Moreover, if they were both identical with Guy Fawkes, they would be identical with each other, which is

also absurd. Hence we could not say that they were both identical with Guy Fawkes. We might instead say that one of them was identical with Guy Fawkes, and that the other was just like him; but this would be an utterly vacuous manoeuvre, since there would be *ex hypothesi* no principle determining which description was to apply to which. So it would be best, if anything, to say that both had mysteriously become like Guy Fawkes, clairvoyantly knew about him, or something like this. If this would be the best description of each of the two, why would it not be the best description of Charles if Charles alone were changed? (113, pp. 238–9)

I think this proves *something*, but not 'that bodily identity is always a necessary condition of personal identity' or, as Williams puts it elsewhere, that to talk of identity in the case in which Charles alone makes the memory-claim 'would be at least quite vacuous'.

Part of the difficulty in seeing what it proves lies in the case being so far-fetched. It has not a basis in what we know, or suspect, about the physical basis of memory, for instance.

Let us see whether we can construct a case in the consideration of which we are not distracted by such thoughts as that Guy Fawkes's memories were somehow stored in Guy Fawkes's head and that there is nothing in Charles's head that was in Guy Fawkes's head. In short, let us not ignore, but actually take account of, what scientists tell us about the physical basis of memory, in constructing our problem case.

(iv) TWO PEOPLE IN ONE BODY?

In his book, *The Bisected Brain*, Michael S. Gazzaniga says what the results are of bisecting the *corpus callosum*, in the middle of the brain:

> Just as conjoined twins are two different people sharing a common body, the callosum-sectioned human has two separate conscious spheres sharing a common brain stem, head and body. . . . A slice of the surgeon's knife through the midline commissures produces two separate, but equal, cognitive systems each with its own abilities to learn, emote, think, and act. (34, pp. 1–2)

In a paper, 'Disconnexion Syndromes in Animals and Man' Norman Geschwind comments on how misleading it is to talk of 'the patient' in cases of disconnexion. He writes that he and a colleague were constantly dealing with questions such as

> 'If he can speak normally and he knows what he's holding in his left hand why can't he tell you?' We had to point out that we couldn't say that 'the patient knew what was in his left hand' and that 'the patient could speak normally' since that part of the patient which could speak normally was not the same part of the patient which 'knew' (non-verbally)

what was in the left hand. This is at first blush an odd way to speak – it is hard not to say 'the patient' and yet it is clear that this terminology is misleading. (36)

The alternative terminology would seem to be one in which we talk of there being two people in one body.

(v) TWO PEOPLE IN ONE BODY, WITH THE SAME MEMORIES?

What is the physical basis of memory? An assumption that might reasonably be made is that when someone learns something there are changes in the electrical properties of the 'synapses' (the junctions between the neurons, or nerve cells) in his brain. Crudely, the circuitry is altered.

The difficulty with this assumption is that alterations in circuitry are presumably in a specific place in the brain, and yet there is experimental evidence that when rats learn to run a maze no brain operation to cut out a small area will destroy the habit (53). It is as if memory is a distributed function of the entire cortex. On the other hand at about the same time as this evidence of the non-localisability of memory traces was appearing, other experiments suggested the opposite. W. Penfield found he could induce his patients to have particular memories by stimulating particular regions of the temporal cortex electrically. Repeated stimulation of the same spot produced the same memory.

An explanation of this apparent contradiction has been given by Steven Rose in terms of 're-dundant coding networks' in the brain. He writes:

> If the same memory is coded in many parts of the cortex; that is, if the state of threshold or synaptic efficacy of a large number of cells, not necessarily, indeed perhaps definitely not, all connected with one another, is altered during the learning process, then the memory may well be stored in many different parts of the system. Particular sets of circuits and firing patterns may form the relevant code, but the memory will not be localised to a single net-work. Rather, it will be duplicated in both brain hemispheres and many times over. Thus cortical ablation of a circumscribed region will not ablate particular memories because duplicate copies are stored elsewhere. None the less, stimulation of any of these particular regions will trigger firing on at least one of the redundant coding networks. Thus the memories invoked by stimulation in Pen-field's experiments become explicable. I do not think that there are any phenomena of memory which cannot be explained by this redundant network / modifiable synapse theory. (90, pp. 208–9)

If the same memories are stored in each of the hemispheres of the brain, and the brain is then bi-sected, and if when a brain has been bisected we talk of there being two people in one body, then it would seem that we ought to talk of two people *with the same memories* in one body.

(vi) TRANSPLANTING A BISECTED BRAIN

The next step in the construction of our problem case is admittedly a rather fanciful one. It is to suppose that just as there can be heart transplants so there can be brain transplants. But instead of a whole brain being transplanted into one body from which the original brain has been removed, the brain is bisected and one half goes into one fresh body, the other into another.

We can graft all this fact and fancy onto Bernard Williams's story about Guy Fawkes, Charles and Robert. On his execution Guy Fawkes's brain is removed, bisected, and the two halves preserved. Later Charles's brain is removed and half of Guy Fawkes's brain put in its place, and Robert's brain is removed and the other half of Guy Fawkes's brain put in its place. Then out of the mouths of *both* 'Charles' *and* 'Robert' come claims to have done the things only Guy Fawkes did.

With this modification of Bernard Williams's story, so as to make it at least a bit less far-fetched, his question becomes the following:

> If there were a bisected brain-transplant (half of Guy Fawkes's brain going into what used to be Charles's body and half into what used to be Robert's body) it would be absurd to say that the two

people were both Guy Fawkes since it is absurd to say that Guy Fawkes is in two places at once and absurd to say that two people are identical with one another. Further, there would be no reason for saying that one, rather than the other, was Guy Fawkes. So if there were a *whole* brain transplant (all of Guy Fawkes's brain going into what used to be Charles's body) would it not be vacuous to say that 'Charles' is now Guy Fawkes?

Why should it be vacuous? What does Bernard Williams require for a personal identity claim to be non-vacuous?

Let us see if we can get help with these questions from Derek Parfit.

(vii) POSTSCRIPT

In the previous section I described the supposition that there can be brain transplants as 'rather fanciful'. I have since read in *The Sunday Times* for 9 December 1973 (p. 13), a report of how a team from the Metropolitan Hospital in Cleveland under Dr R. J. White have successfully transplanted a monkey's head onto another monkey's body. Dr White is reported as having said, 'Technically a human head transplant is possible', and as hoping that 'it may be possible eventually to transplant *parts* of the brain or other organs inside the head'.

7. IS BELIEF IN THE SPECIAL NATURE OF PERSONAL IDENTITY FALSE?

(i) PARFIT'S ANSWER TO THE BISECTED BRAIN TRANSPLANT QUESTION

In a paper (73) and in a radio discussion I had with him (74) Derek Parfit has questioned what he describes as the 'belief in the special nature of personal identity'. One way of saying what this belief is is in terms of the bisected brain transplant case I outlined in the last chapter. Suppose the question is asked: If half of Guy Fawkes's brain were transplanted into what used to be Charles's body and half into what used to be Robert's body, so that out of the mouths of *both* 'Charles' *and* 'Robert' came claims to have done the things only Guy Fawkes did, would Guy Fawkes (a) not survive, (b) survive in the body of one of the two, or (c) survive in the bodies of both? The belief in the special nature of personal identity can be expressed as the belief that this question about Guy Fawkes must have one of the three answers suggested. In more general terms it can be expressed as follows: 'Whatever happens between now and any future time, either I shall still exist, or I shall not. Any future experience will either be *my* experience, or it will not' (73, p. 3). Parfit's reasons for rejecting the three answers suggested are as follows.

(a) If the *whole* of Guy Fawkes's brain were transplanted into what used to be Charles's body, so that out of the mouth of 'Charles' came claims to have done the things only Guy Fawkes did, we would regard that as a case of Guy Fawkes having survived. (Parfit is here taking things in the reverse order to that taken by Williams.) Equally, if *half* of Guy Fawkes's brain were destroyed and the other half transplanted into what used to be Charles's body, so that out of 'Charles's' mouth came claims to have done the things only Guy Fawkes did, we would regard that as a case of Guy Fawkes having survived. (People have in fact survived with half their brains destroyed.) But in that case how could we deny that Guy Fawkes had survived if the other half were not destroyed but successfully transplanted into what used to be Robert's body? 'How could a double success be a failure?' (73, p. 5).

(b) The objection to the second answer – that Guy Fawkes survived in the body of one of the two, but not in that of the other – is that there may be no more reason to say he survives in 'Charles's' body than in 'Robert's'. Both, equally, may seem, to themselves and to others, to be Guy Fawkes. And if there is nothing to choose between them, surely it is implausible to say that Guy Fawkes survives in one but not in the other.

(c) The third answer is that Guy Fawkes survives in *both* 'Charles's' and 'Robert's' bodies. With this answer it looks as if we have to say *either* that one person has become two different people *or* that one person has acquired two different bodies. But we cannot say either of these things. To say the first is to say that two things that are not identical with one another are both identical with a third thing. And to say the second would be intolerable. After the bisected brain transplant operation the two 'products' would 'each have all the attributes of a person. They could live at opposite ends of the earth. (If they later met, they might even fail to recognize each other.) It would become intolerable to deny that they were different people' (73, p. 7).

Parfit, then, rejects all three of the suggested answers to the bisected brain transplant question. His own account of the situation is in terms of what he calls 'psychological continuity'. The two 'products' of transplanting half of Guy Fawkes's brain into each of two bodies are 'psychologically continuous' with Guy Fawkes. If there had been only one 'product' we could have described the situation in terms of identity. As it is we cannot. But it does not matter. What matters is 'psychological continuity', which may take either a one-one or a one-many (branching) form. We talk of 'identity' when it takes a one-one form. The 'belief in the special nature of personal identity' can now be re-described. It is the belief that there is more to personal identity than non-branching psychological continuity.

(ii) THE BEARING OF PARFIT'S ANSWER ON WILLIAMS'S QUESTION

Given that we understand what 'psychological continuity' is, it now becomes possible to answer

Bernard Williams's question. The question was: If the best description of Charles and Robert, who both claim to remember doing the things Guy Fawkes did, is 'to say that both had mysteriously become like Guy Fawkes, clairvoyantly knew about him, or something like this . . . why would it not be the best description of Charles if Charles alone were changed?' Parfit's answer to this question would be: Because in the case of Charles alone being changed the psychological continuity is non-branching.

For Williams, on the other hand, to say that Charles is identical with Guy Fawkes would be 'quite vacuous'. An explanation of this would be that Williams, unlike Parfit, thinks there *is* more to personal identity than non-branching psychological continuity. Williams could be represented as holding that it would be quite vacuous to talk of personal identity if there were nothing more to it than non-branching psychological continuity.

Parfit refers to another paper by Williams (111, p. 44) in which he puts forward the principle that an important judgement should be asserted and denied only on importantly different grounds. Parfit writes:

> Williams applied this principle to a case in which one man is psychologically continuous with the dead Guy Fawkes, and a case in which two men are. His argument was this. If we treat psychological continuity as a sufficient ground for speaking of identity, we

shall say that the one man is Guy Fawkes. But we could not say that the two men are, although we should have the same ground. This disobeys the principle. The remedy is to deny that the one man is Guy Fawkes, to insist that sameness of the body is necessary for identity. (73, p. 13)

Parfit's own view would be that by comparison with a judgement about psychological continuity a judgement about personal identity is not an important judgement. By saying that Charles is identical with Guy Fawkes we merely mark the fact that the psychological continuity is one-one (non-branching). So there is no need to fall back on the reactionary position that bodily identity is a necessary condition of personal identity.

(iii) 'PSYCHOLOGICAL CONTINUITY' AND THE UNITY QUESTION

For me, the most disturbing thing about Parfit's answer to the bisected brain transplant question is that it seems to bring us round full circle to where we began. We began with the Unity Question. After trying a succession of more and more implausible answers to it we settled, provisionally, on the obvious answer: that two experiences are the same person's experiences if they are experiences had by the same person. But this answer to the Unity Question is satisfactory only if we have a satisfactory answer to the question 'What do we mean by "the same person"?' (the Identity Question). If Parfit is right, then to understand what is meant by 'the same person' we have to understand what is meant by 'psychological continuity'. And the question 'What is psychological continuity?' sounds suspiciously like the question 'What is the unity of the mind?' That is, it sounds suspiciously like the sort of question that we might expect to find answered in terms of causal relations between earlier and later experiences. Have we come all this way only to find ourselves back where we started, in Hume's labyrinth?

Evidently we shall have to examine fairly carefully what Parfit means by 'psychological continuity'.

(iv) MEMORY AND QUASI-MEMORY

We have seen, on reflecting on how we distinguish real memory from seeming memory, that memory presupposes personal identity. Just as 'p is true' is a condition of 'I know p' being true, so 'I am X' is a condition of 'I (really) remember doing what only X did' being true.

Parfit accepts this. Accepting it, and holding that personal identity is to be analysed in terms of psychological continuity (we speak of 'identity' when there is one-one, or non-branching, psychological continuity), he cannot go on to analyse psychological continuity in terms of memory. To do so would be circular.

Accordingly he introduces the concept of quasi-memory (q-memory, for short), and analyses psychological continuity in terms of it, and of other q-things, such as q-intentions. He avoids the circularity of analysing psychological continuity in terms of something that presupposes personal identity by defining q-memory in such a way that it is not a logical truth that we can q-remember only our own experiences.

He then analyses (real) memory in terms of q-memory. 'Memories are, simply, q-memories of one's own experiences' (73, p. 16).

He holds that 'we misinterpret what it is to remember' (p. 11). I think he means that we mistakenly think that the sort of memory that presupposes personal identity is the basic concept. He says that it is easy to believe that the description of memory *must* refer to identity, and that 'this belief about memory is an important cause of the view that personal identity has a special nature' (p. 14). Presumably he means that the description of memory *need not* refer to identity; that is, that we could have started with the concept of q-memory and then built up, from it, the concept of memory by imposing a restriction. When the restriction is imposed the reference to identity is explicit: memories are q-memories of *one's own* experiences. But with recognition that q-memory is the basic concept, the fact that memory involves identity need not worry him.

If I am right about this then Parfit has to show that q-memory could be our basic concept; that is, that we could have had the concept of q-memory without having the concept of memory.

(v) THE DEFINITION OF Q-MEMORY

Parfit defines *q*-memory as follows:

> I am *q*-remembering an experience if (1)
> I have a belief about a past experience which
> seems in itself like a memory belief, (2)
> someone did have such an experience, and (3)
> my belief is dependent upon this experience
> in the same way (whatever that is) in which a
> memory of an experience is dependent upon
> it. (73, p. 15)

Before considering whether *q*-memory, so defined,
could be our basic concept, let us try to understand the definition.

It is not difficult to imagine circumstances in
which the first two conditions might be met. A
friend and I are told that if we take a certain drug,
while thinking hard of one another, then until the
effects of the drug have worn off (mercifully after
only a few days) we will be so well aware, by telepathy, of what is going on in each other's minds
that I may mistake a telepathically-received
memory of a past experience of my friend for a
memory of a past experience of my own, and vice
versa.

There is a problem about what Parfit means by
the third condition. It might be argued that the way
in which a memory of an experience is dependent
upon it is precisely by being a *memory* of it. Par-

fit can hardly mean this, for if he did there would be no difference between *q*-memory and memory.

I think he must mean that the past experience *causes* me to have a belief about it. It causes me to have a belief about it in the same way (whatever that is) in which a past experience causes me to have a memory-belief about it. Again, he cannot mean to restrict the causal way to that which operates in real memory. For one thing, he wants his account to embrace the case in which my brain is half that of Guy Fawkes. (I cannot then say that the experience I *q*-remember is *my* past experience, since someone else may be in a position to say the same, and two different people cannot be identical with one and the same person.) Another case he wants his account to embrace is that in which a record of an experience, in someone else's brain, is somehow reproduced in mine. (We can even suppose that this is how telepathy works.) He describes a case of brain-state reproduction which deserves special mention.

(vi) 'A SECULAR VERSION OF THE
  RESURRECTION'

The following is an extract from the radio discussion I had with Parfit:

PARFIT: Suppose that the following is going to happen to me. When I die in a normal way, scientists are going to map the states of all the cells in my brain and body and after a few months they will have constructed a perfect duplicate of me out of organic matter. And this duplicate will wake up fully psychologically continuous with me, seeming to remember my life with my character, and so on.

VESEY: Yes.

PARFIT: Now, in this case, which is a secular version of the Resurrection, we're very in-inclined to think that the following question arises and is very real and very important. The question is: 'Will that person who wakes up in, say, three months be me or will he be some quite other person who's merely artificially made to be exactly like me?'

VESEY: It does seem to be a real question. I mean, in the one case, if it is going to be me then I have expectations, and so on, and in the other case, where it isn't me, I don't.

PARFIT: I agree. It seems as if there couldn't be a bigger difference between it being me and it being someone else.

VESEY: But you want to say that the two possibilities are in fact the same?

PARFIT: I want to say that those two descriptions – 'It's going to be me', and 'It's going to be someone who is merely exactly like me'– don't describe different outcomes, different courses of events, only one of which can happen. They are two ways of describing one and the same course of events. (74)

This case of brain-state reproduction deserves special mention, I think, because of its relevance for the interpretation of Parfit's third condition for my *q*-remembering an experience. Suppose I am the person whom scientists have constructed out of organic matter. Provided they have done a perfect job of mapping the brain and body cells of someone who died some months ago, and reproducing them in organic matter, I shall be psychologically continuous with the dead person. Therefore, I shall be able to *q*-remember the dead person's experiences. Therefore, when I *q*-remember such an experience, the belief I have about it will be dependent upon the dead person's past experience in the same way as his memory-belief would have been dependent upon it if he had lived and remembered it. In short, by the 'dependence' mentioned in the third condition for my *q*-remembering an experience, Parfit means no more than that there is a perfect duplication, in me, brought about either naturally or artificially, of the brain-state corresponding to the original experience. And, since there is no theoretical limit to the number of times something can be duplicated, any number of people may *q*-remember the dead person's experiences. Conversely, the dead person, before he dies, if he knows what is going to happen, can *q*-expect experiences to be had by any number of duplicates of himself.

Parfit supposes the scientists to construct a *perfect* duplicate of me. But we can readily imagine that they fail to map *all* the cells in my brain and body, or fail to construct a duplicate that accords entirely with what they have mapped, or both. Then, I suppose, some near-duplicate of me might seem to remember an experience I had not in fact had. Would he q-remember it, on Parfit's definition? It depends on how we interpret his second condition. ('I am q-remembering an experience if . . . (2) someone did have such an experience'). If the 'someone' has to be the person the scientists intended to duplicate perfectly then the near-duplicate does not q-remember the experience he seems to remember. If there is not this restriction then the experience the near-duplicate seems to remember would have to be one never had by *anyone* for it not to be q-remembered. It would become impossible to determine whether or not an experience the near-duplicate seemed to remember was genuinely q-remembered. Even the restriction to the person the scientists intended to duplicate would mean that the near-duplicate would not know ninety-nine times out of a hundred whether he was really q-remembering an experience or merely seeming to q-remember it.

(vii) A JUST STANDARD FOR DECIDING DISPUTES?

At the end of Chapter 4 I suggested that the reason why Hume came to have misgivings about his own theory was that it left him with 'no just standard by which we can decide any dispute' concerning identity (42, p. 262). This was because causal relations 'may diminish by insensible degrees'.

Are we any better off with Parfit than we were with Hume? If personal identity is nothing more than non-branching psychological continuity, have we a 'just standard by which we can decide any dispute'?

Unless I have grossly misinterpreted Parfit's third condition for my *q*-remembering an experience we are no better off with Parfit than we were with Hume. If anything, we are worse off.

8. OUT OF THE LABYRINTH?

(i) REVIEW

Our route can be compared with that taken by Hume.

Hume began by rejecting the view of 'some philosophers, who imagine we are every moment intimately conscious of what we call our SELF'. He rejected it in favour of the view of 'most philosophers', namely, 'that personal identity *arises* from consciousness'. This seemed to him 'a promising aspect' of his approach. But in the end it led to his giving an account which would mean our having 'no just standard by which we can decide any dispute' about identity.

We began by distinguishing the Unity Question and the Identity Question. We rejected an argument, Russell's, for our being 'acquainted with something which we call "I"' and, thereby, the answer to the Unity Question that a succession of experiences are the same person's if they are related to one and the same self-conscious self. For us, a promising aspect was the thought that all we need to do to answer the Unity Question is to say what we mean by 'the same person'. At first it seemed that this would be easy, for it seemed to be a rule that personal identity and bodily identity should go hand in hand. But then it appeared that situations (bisected brain transplant cases) were imaginable to deal with which we would either, fol-

lowing Bernard Williams, have to say that bodily
identity is a necessary condition of personal
identity (i.e. not allow exceptions to the rule), or,
following Derek Parfit, forsake the rule, and say
that personal identity is non-branching psychological continuity, analysable in terms of q-memory,
etc. The first of these courses seems unreasonable,
as Parfit points out. But if we take the second
course we seem to end up with no more just a standard by which to decide disputes about identity
than Hume was able to find. Indeed, like Hume's,
the standard with which we are left is one which
requires our making shaky speculations about
causal connexions to decide disputes about something we do not ordinarily think of as a causal
matter at all.

On the other hand there is a significant difference between the way in which causal connexions
are reached on Hume's route and the way they are
reached on our route. On our route they are reached via the thought that memory has a 'physical
basis'. But there is nothing of this in Hume.
Memory does figure in his account, but it is either
as the source of resemblance among perceptions
(for memory is 'but a faculty, by which we raise
up the images of past perceptions' and 'an image
necessarily resembles its object') or as the means
of discovering 'the relation of cause and effect
among our different perceptions' (42, pp. 260,
262).

The thought that memory has a physical basis
arose in connexion with the question whether
Charles, who makes memory-claims that fit the

pattern of Guy Fawkes's life, is identical with Guy Fawkes. The supposition seems far-fetched, it was suggested, because it does not accord with what we know, or suspect, about the physical basis of memory. It was this suggestion that led to a consideration of the bisected brain transplant cases, and, eventually, to the proposition that personal identity is no more than non-branching psychological continuity analysable in terms of q-memory, etc.

(ii) RECONSIDERATIONS

Let us reconsider. Is it really because of what we know, or suspect, about the physical basis of memory that the supposition that Charles is identical with Guy Fawkes seems far-fetched? Is it not, rather, simply because Guy Fawkes, on our ordinary reckoning of these matters, is long-since dead and buried whereas Charles is alive and before us?

Once we allow ourselves to be weaned away just a little from our 'ordinary reckonings' it is difficult to draw the line. Let us reconsider the whole brain transplant case. It would surely be unreasonable, we allow ourselves to be persuaded, not to say that the person with X's brain, who claims to remember doing what X did, etc., is X. Yes, it would be unreasonable – in the light of *part* of our ordinary reckoning of these matters. The trouble is that, having allowed that the person with X's brain is X, we conveniently forget that this does violence to another part of our ordinary reckoning, though if there actually were a brain transplant we would constantly have to be explaining what had happened to people not in the know. We forget all this, and, when we are philosophising, go on to talk as if the part of our ordinary reckoning to which the decision to say that the person with X's brain is X does violence had been shown to be irrelevant to our concept of personal identity. The brain, carrying with it as it does the memory, becomes all-important in our new reckoning.

It is no time at all before we are seriously considering candidates for personal identity that on our ordinary reckoning we would never have considered. Let us reconsider 'a secular version of the Resurrection'. Suppose scientists do as Parfit suggests. That is, they 'map the states of all the cells in my brain and body' and construct 'a perfect duplicate of me out of organic matter'. But suppose they do it while I am still alive. Certainly people might mistake the duplicate for me, just as they sometimes mistake identical twins for one another. But there is nothing in this to tempt me to say I am identical with the duplicate, any more than there is a temptation to say that identical twins are numerically identical. Why, then, should there be a temptation to say this if I drop dead just as the duplicate is brought to life?

Parfit would say that the duplicate is 'fully psychologically continuous with me, seeming to remember my life, with my character, and so on'. If I have understood him rightly, he is committed to saying that since this is a case of non-branching psychological continuity the duplicate *is me*. But on our ordinary reckoning it is, plainly, not me – in spite of seeming to remember having done things I have done, etc. Parfit has cut the last string connecting his understanding of personal identity with our ordinary understanding of it. And in so doing he has delivered himself into a labyrinth of Humean proportions.

(iii) WITTGENSTEIN ON PERSONAL IDENTITY

Why is the concept of personal identity so labyrinth-prone? Is there no just standard by which we can decide disputes? Wittgenstein writes:

> Our actual use of the phrase 'the same person' and of the name of a person is based on the fact that many characteristics which we use as the criteria for identity coincide in the vast majority of cases. . . . This can best be seen by imagining unreal cases which show us what different 'geometries' we would be inclined to use if facts were different. . . . Imagine a man whose memories on the even days of his life comprise the events of all these days, skipping entirely what happened on the odd days. On the other hand, he remembers on an odd day what happened on previous odd days, but his memory then skips the even days without a feeling of discontinuity. If we like we can also assume that he has alternating appearances and characteristics on odd and even days. Are we bound to say that here two persons are inhabiting the same

body? That is, is it right to say that there are, and wrong to say that there aren't, or vice versa? Neither. For the *ordinary* use of the word 'person' is what one might call a composite use suitable under the ordinary circumstances. If I assume, as I do, that these circumstances are changed, the application of the term 'person' or 'personality' has thereby changed; and if I wish to preserve this term and give it a use analogous to its former use, I am at liberty to choose between many uses, that is, between many different kinds of analogy. One might say in such a case that the term 'personality' hasn't got one legitimate heir only. (118, pp. 61–2)

(iv) TRACTATUS 2.0211–2 AND THE LOGIC OF THE LANGUAGE OF EXPERIENCE

Wittgenstein's treatment of the problems of personal identity is like his treatment of the Other Minds problem. In his account of the concept of 'person' as in his account of the concept of 'pain' he claims that one proposition's having the sense it has depends on another proposition's being true. This is a revolution in his thought – arguably *the* revolution (109), for the picture theory of meaning was central in his view of the relation of language and reality in the *Tractatus*, and there he wrote:

> If the world had no substance, then whether a proposition had sense would depend on whether another proposition was true.

It would then be impossible to form a picture of the world (true or false).

(119, 2.0211–12)

A simple example will serve to illustrate what it is for the sense of one proposition to depend on the truth of another. We use such time-of-day expressions as 'It's morning', 'It's afternoon', 'It's night'. But if it were not the case that the earth revolves on its axis, so that places on the earth have varying positions relative to the sun, we would have no use for them. Our having a use for them – i.e. their having sense – depends on its being true that the earth revolves, etc. To say it is afternoon at some place is to say that at that place the sun is past the zenith but not yet over the horizon.

I shall call this a 'fact-presupposing' explanation of the meaning of time-of-day expressions. It provides an answer to the question 'How can I mean anything by "It's afternoon"?'.

Someone who could not see what this question was getting at might give what may be called an 'experiential' explanation. This might be in terms of his experience of seeing the sun more than half-way across the sky.

Consider now, the question 'How can I mean anything by the word "toothache"?'. Two, opposed, experiential explanations readily occur to us. One is in terms of 'the feeling of toothache itself'. The other is in terms of people looking, sounding, etc., as if they have toothache.

Wittgenstein is opposed to *both* the experiential explanations. His own, fact-presupposing, explanation is in terms of people moaning and crying when they are in pain, and of a child learning to use expressions like 'I have a toothache' to replace its moans (115, p. 295; 117, part I, § 244). The linguistic expression 'stands for', 'is a substitute for' the natural expression (115, p. 301). If he did not naturally groan, grimace, etc., then, says Wittgenstein, 'it would be impossible to teach a child the use of the word "tooth-ache"' (117, part I, § 257). 'The game we play with the word "toothache" entirely depends upon there being a behaviour which we call the expression of toothache' (115, p. 290).

I have considered elsewhere (107) the relevance for the Other Minds problem of how we acquire the language of experience. Its relevance for the problem of personal identity is twofold. First, by exhibiting the internal relation between the natural expression of pain and the language in which we talk of pain, it makes it clear *why* the question 'Whose feeling of pain do the tears that are streaming down Jones's cheeks express?' (see p. 75 above) is so absurd. Second, it is a further example of how the meaningfulness of talk about something is conditional on certain facts being as they are. In the case of talk of pain the fact is that people naturally moan and cry when they are in pain, and others react to them with sympathy. In the case of talk of 'the same person' the fact is that, as Wittgenstein puts it, 'many characteristics which we use as the criteria for identity coincide in the vast majority of cases'.

(v) THE MATERIALS OF HUME'S LABYRINTH

Hume's labyrinth, I suggest, is made of three materials, only one of which is sound. The unsound materials are those provided by Dualism and Empiricism.

The material provided by Dualism is the notion that a person is distinct from his body. It is this material that makes the problem of personal identity, for Hume, one of how perceptions are united.

The material provided by Empiricism is the notion that the explanation of the meaning of an expression must be an experiential one. It is this that prevents Hume from seeing the significance of his own remark that 'self or person is not any one impression, but that to which our several impressions and ideas are suppos'd to have a reference' (42, p. 251). Certainly, when I say 'I am acquainted with this sense-datum' I am not acquainted with two things, my self as well as the sense-datum. But, then, I do not need to be, to use 'I' perfectly properly.

The only sound material in the labyrinth is the one to which Wittgenstein draws attention when he says that 'the *ordinary* use of the word "person" is what one might call a composite use suitable under the ordinary circumstances'. There are various ways of putting this. To say that there is nothing *essential* about personal identity, or that the self is not a *substance*, is to suggest that there *is* something essential about other things, or that other things *are* substances. To say that there is no just standard by which we can decide any dispute about identity is, surely, wrong. We can decide ordinary disputes – in the way in which we do. To say that the belief that whatever happens between now and any future time, either I shall still exist, or I shall not, is false, is confusing. It suggests that a question *about* a concept (If this were to happen would our ordinary concept of personal identity still be applicable?) is the same as a question *employing* a concept (If this were to happen would there still exist someone identical with X?).

The sound material, by itself, does not constitute a labyrinth. Unsound material, of one sort or another, has to be added. It is up to us not to add it.

NOTES ON READING

Chapter 1

In Hume's *Treatise* (42) read Book I, Part IV, Section VI, and the related note in the Appendix, beginning 'I had entertain'd some hopes . . .'. There are many references to Hume's views on personal identity in the literature. Three of the best articles are by Pears (76), Penelhum (77), and Butchvarov (13), but Norman Kemp Smith's commentary (104, pp. 96–9, 497–505) should not be ignored.

To get the feel of the Unity Question look at Broad (11, ch. XIII), Beloff (8, ch. VI), Lewis (57, chs X–XII), and Evans (29, chs 6, 7). Both Lewis and Evans write on the relation between the Unity Question and the Identity Question – or, rather, on the relation between the concepts of Self and Person – taking a view that is opposed to that of this book.

Chapter 2

What I say about Berkeley is based on Brown (12), and about Kant, on Paton (75).

A good introduction to the neutral monism of Russell's *Analysis of Mind* is James (44), and there are useful discussions of the theory in Broad (11, pp. 578–84) and Ayer (3, pp. 110–21).

I do not know of any discussions of 'here'. On the other hand, many philosophers have written on 'I', among them Schlick (94), Aldrich (1), Wittgenstein (references in the text), Ryle (93, ch. 6), Ramsey (87), Geach (references in the text), Strawson (106, ch. 3), Shoemaker (100, pp. 9–18, 50–2, 91, 126–7) and Hartnack (40). Shoemaker's *Self-Knowledge and Self-*

Identity is worth reading on all the issues that arise under the heading of 'personal identity'.

Chapter 3

It is interesting, having read Jones's 1949 paper (48) to read his very different 1967 paper (46).

There are discussions of James's theory in Scott (95), Capek (16), and Ayer (5, pp. 263–88).

Chapter 4

In Locke's *Essay* (59) read Book II, ch. 27, and in Reid's *Essays on the Intellectual Powers of Man* (88) read Essay III, chs 4 and 6. Grice (38) and Quinton (86) are, on the whole, in sympathy with Locke. Flew (30) is not. Flew's article marks a turning point in discussions of personal identity.

Chapter 5

On Descartes's reasons for not giving the obvious answer to the Unity Question, read Descartes (24, pp. 61–75, 109–24, 274–82) and Kim (50). On Ayer's reasons read Strawson (106. ch. 3) and, of course, Ayer (4, ch. 4).

Chapters 6 and 7

The following is a selection from the work that has been published fairly recently on such questions as 'Is bodily identity a necessary condition of personal identity?', 'Could memory provide a sufficient condition of personal identity?' and 'Can sense be given to talk of disembodied existence?': Chisholm (18), Chisholm and Shoemaker (19), Coburn (20), Daniels (22), Greenwood (37), Hardie (39), Lewy (58), Long (60), Miri (69), Odegard (71), Palma (72),

Penelhum (78, 79, 80), Price (81), Pucetti (85), Shaffer (96), Shoemaker (97–102), Shorter (103), Williams (111–14).

Williams (114) and Wiggins (110) discuss issues discussed by Parfit (73) in Chapter 7. A useful introduction to Wiggins's book, which is not easy, is Shoemaker's review of it (102).

Chapter 8

Read Wittgenstein (118, pp. 61–72). On Section (iv) see White (109) and Vesey (107).

BIBLIOGRAPHY

In this bibliography are listed the works referred to in the text and Notes on Reading, and also some further works the selection of which reflects the main concerns of the book.

1. Aldrich, V. C., 'Messrs. Schlick and Ayer on Immortality', *Philosophical Review*, 47 (1938) pp. 209–13.
2. Alexander, S., *Space, Time, and Deity* (Macmillan, London, 1920).
3. Ayer, A. J., *Russell and Moore: The Analytical Heritage* (Macmillan, London, 1971; paperback edn 1973).
4. Ayer, A. J., *The Concept of a Person and Other Essays* (Macmillan, London, 1963; paperback edn 1973).
5. Ayer, A. J., *The Origins of Pragmatism: Studies in the Philosophy of Charles Sanders Peirce and William James* (Macmillan, London, 1968).
6. Ayer, A. J., *The Problem of Knowledge* (Macmillan, London, 1956).
7. Beloff, J., Review of I. Stevenson, *Twenty Cases Suggestive of Reincarnation*, in *Journal of the Society for Psychical Research*, 44 (1967) pp. 88–94.
8. Beloff, J., *The Existence of Mind* (MacGibbon & Kee, London, 1962).
9. Bennett, J., 'The Simplicity of the Soul', *Journal of Philosophy*, 64 (1967) pp. 648–60.
10. Berkeley, G., *A New Theory of Vision and Other Writings*, Everyman's Library No. 483 (Dent, London, 1910).
11. Broad, C. D., *The Mind and its Place in Nature* (Routledge & Kegan Paul, London, 1925).

12. Brown, S. C., 'Berkeley on the Unity of the Self', in *Reason and Reality*, Royal Institute of Philosophy Lectures, 5, 1970–1 (Macmillan, London, 1972) pp. 64–87.

13. Butchvarov, P., 'The Self and Perceptions: A Study in Humean Philosophy', *Philosophical Quarterly*, 9 (1959) pp. 97–115.

14. Butler, J., 'Of Personal Identity', *Butler's Analogy of Religion*, ed. W. E. Gladstone (O.U.P., London, 1896) pp. 345–54.

15. Campbell, C. A., *On Selfhood and Godhood* (Allen & Unwin, London, 1957).

16. Capek, M., 'The Reappearance of the Self in the Last Philosophy of William James', *Philosophical Review*, 62 (1953) pp. 526–44.

17. Chandler, H. S., 'Shoemaker's Arguments against Locke', *Philosophical Quarterly*, 19 (1969) pp. 263–5.

18. Chisholm, R., 'On the Observability of the Self', *Philosophy and Phenomenological Research*, 30 (1969) pp. 7–21.

19. Chisholm, R., and Shoemaker, S., 'The Loose and Popular and the Strict and the Philosophical Senses of Identity', *Perception and Personal Identity: Proceedings of the 1967 Oberlin Colloquium in Philosophy*, ed. N. Care, and R. H. Grimm (Press of Case Western Reserve Univ., Cleveland, 1969).

20. Coburn, R. C., 'Bodily Continuity and Personal Identity', *Analysis*, 20 (1960) pp. 117–20.

21. Cook, J. W., 'Human Beings', *Studies in the Philosophy of Wittgenstein*, ed. P. Winch (Routledge & Kegan Paul, London, 1969) pp. 117–51.

22. Daniels, C. B., 'Personal Identity', *American Philosophical Quarterly*, 6 (1969) pp. 226–32.

23. Descartes, R., *Philosophical Works*, trans. E. S. Haldane and G. R. T. Ross (C.U.P., London, 1934).

24. Descartes, R., *Philosophical Writings*, trans. E.

Anscombe, and P. T. Geach (Nelson, London, 1954).

25. Dorward, A., 'The Nature of the Self and of Self-Consciousness', *Aristotelian Society Supplementary Volume*, 8 (1928) pp. 214–21.

26. Ducasse, C. J., *The Belief in a Life after Death* (Charles C. Thomas, Illinois, 1961).

27. Duhrssen, A., 'The Self and the Body', *Review of Metaphysics*, 10 (1956) pp. 28–34.

28. Eccles, J. C., *The Brain and the Unity of Conscious Experience* (C.U.P., London, 1965).

29. Evans, C. O., *The Subject of Consciousness* (Allen & Unwin, London, 1970).

30. Flew, A. G. N., 'Locke and the Problem of Personal Identity', *Philosophy*, 26 (1951) pp. 53–68.

31. Flew, A. G. N., 'Selves', *Mind*, 63 (1949) pp. 355–8.

32. Flew, A. G. N., ' "The Soul" of Mr. A. M. Quinton', *Journal of Philosophy*, 60 (1963) pp. 337–44.

33. Gallie, I., 'Mental Facts', *Proceedings Aristotelian Society*, 37 (1936–7) pp. 191–212.

34. Gazzaniga, M. S., *The Bisected Brain* (Appleton-Century-Crofts, New York, 1970).

35. Geach, P. T., *Mental Acts* (Routledge & Kegan Paul, London, 1957).

36. Geschwind, N., 'Disconnexion Syndromes in Animals and Man', *Brain*, 88 (1965) pp. 636–9.

37. Greenwood, T., 'Personal Identity and Memory', *Philosophical Quarterly*, 17 (1967) pp. 334–44.

38. Grice, H. P., 'Personal Identity', *Mind*, 50 (1941) pp. 330–50.

39. Hardie, W. F. R., 'Bodies and Minds', *The Listener* (4 April 1960) pp. 655–7.

40. Hartnack, J., 'The Metaphysics of the "I" ', *Philosophical Quarterly*, 22 (1972) pp. 248–54.

41. Hicks, G. D., 'The Nature of the Self and of Self-Consciousness', *Aristotelian Society Supplementary Volume*, 8 (1928) pp. 189–202.

42. Hume, D., *A Treatise of Human Nature*, ed. L. A. Selby-Bigge (O.U.P., Oxford, 1888).
43. Huxley, T. H., *Hume* (Macmillan, London, 1887).
44. James, William, 'Does Consciousness Exist?', *Essays in Radical Empiricism* (Longmans, London, 1912).
45. James, William, *Principles of Psychology* (Macmillan, London, 1891).
46. Jones, J. R., 'How Do I Know Who I Am?', *Aristotelian Society Supplementary Volume*, 41 (1967) pp. 1–18.
47. Jones, J. R., 'Self-Knowledge', *Aristotelian Society Supplementary Volume*, 30 (1956) pp. 120–42.
48. Jones, J. R., 'The Self in Sensory Cognition', *Mind*, 63 (1949) pp. 40–61.
49. Kant, I., *Critique of Pure Reason*, trans. N. K. Smith (Macmillan, London, 1933).
50. Kim, C.-T., 'Cartesian Dualism and the Unity of the Mind', *Mind*, 80 (1971) pp. 337–53.
51. Knox, J., 'Can the Self Survive the Death of its Mind?', *Religious Studies*, 5 (1969) pp. 85–97.
52. Laird, J., 'The Nature of the Self and of Self-Consciousness', *Aristotelian Society Supplementary Volume*, 8 (1928) pp. 203–13.
53. Lashley, K. S., *Brain Mechanisms and Intelligence* (Univ. Press, Chicago, 1929).
54. Laslett, P. (ed.), *The Physical Basis of Mind* (Basil Blackwell, Oxford, 1950).
55. Lewis, C. I., 'Some Logical Considerations concerning the Mental', *Journal of Philosophy*, 38 (1941) pp. 225–33.
56. Lewis, H. D., 'Mind and Body – Some Observations on Mr. Strawson's Views', *Proceedings Aristotelian Society*, 63 (1962–3) pp. 1–22.
57. Lewis, H. D., *The Elusive Mind* (Allen & Unwin, London, 1969).
58. Lewy, C., 'Is the Notion of Disembodied Exist-

ence Self-Contradictory?', *Proceedings Aristotelian Society*, 43 (1942–3) pp. 59–78.

59. Locke, J., *An Essay concerning Human Understanding*, ed. A. S. Pringle-Pattison (O.U.P., Oxford, 1924).

60. Long, D., 'Philosophical Concept of a Human Body', *Philosophical Review*, 73 (1964) pp. 321–37.

61. Mace, C. A., 'Self-identity', *Aristotelian Society Supplementary Volume*, 18 (1939) pp. 31–48.

62. Mach, E., *The Analysis of Sensations* (Dover, New York, 1959).

63. McDougall, W., *Body and Mind* (Methuen, London, 1911).

64. McTaggart, J. McT. E., *The Nature of Existence* (C.U.P., Cambridge, 1927).

65. Miles, T. R., 'Self-Knowledge', *Aristotelian Society Supplementary Volume*, 30 (1956) pp. 143–56.

66. Mill, J. S., *Examination of Sir William Hamilton's Philosophy*, 6th edn. (Longmans, London, 1889).

67. Milne, A. A., *Winnie-the-Pooh* and *The House at Pooh Corner* (Reprint Society, London, 1957).

68. Minkus, P., *Philosophy of the Person* (Basil Blackwell, Oxford, 1960).

69. Miri, M., 'Memory and Personal Identity', *Mind*, 82 (1973) pp. 1–21.

70. Moore, G. E., 'Wittgenstein's Lectures in 1930–33', *Mind*, 63 (1954) pp. 1–15, 289–316, and 64 (1955) pp. 1–27.

71. Odegard, D., 'Persons and Bodies', *Philosophy and Phenomenological Research*, 31 (1970) pp. 225–42.

72. Palma, A. B., 'Memory and Personal Identity', *Australasian Journal of Philosophy*, 42 (1964) pp. 53–68.

73. Parfit, D., 'Personal Identity', *Philosophical Review*, 80 (1971) pp. 3–27.

74. Parfit, D., 'Personal Identity', *Philosophy in the Open*, ed. Godfrey Vesey (The Open University Press, 1974).

75. Paton, H. J., 'Self-identity', *Mind*, 38 (1929) pp. 312–29.

76. Pears, D. F., 'Hume on Personal Identity', *David Hume: A Symposium*, ed. D. F. Pears (Macmillan, London, 1966; St. Martin's Press, New York, 1966) pp. 43–54.

77. Penelhum, T., 'Hume on Personal Identity', *Philosophical Review*, 64 (1955) pp. 571–89.

78. Penelhum, T., 'Personal Identity', *Encyclopedia of Philosophy*, ed. P. Edwards (The Macmillan Co. of New York and Free Press, New York, 1967).

79. Penelhum, T., 'Personal Identity, Memory and Survival, *Journal of Philosophy*, 56 (1959) pp. 882–903.

80. Penelhum, T., *Survival and Disembodied Existence* (Routledge & Kegan Paul, London, 1970).

81. Price, H. H., 'Survival and the Idea of "Another World",' *Brain and Mind*, ed. J. R. Smythies (Routledge & Kegan Paul, London, 1965) pp. 1–33.

82. Pringle-Pattison, A. S., *The Idea of Immortality* (O.U.P., Oxford, 1922).

83. Prior, A. N., 'Opposite Number', *Review of Metaphysics*, 11 (1957–8) pp. 196–201.

84. Prior, A. N., 'Time, Existence and Identity', *Proceedings Aristotelian Society*, 57 (1965–6) pp. 183–92.

85. Pucetti, R., 'Brain Transplantation and Personal Identity', *Analysis*, 29 (1969) pp. 65–77.

86. Quinton, A. M., 'The Soul', *Journal of Philosophy*, 59 (1962) pp. 393–409.

87. Ramsey, I. T., 'The Systematic Elusiveness of "I"', *Philosophical Quarterly*, 5 (1955) pp. 193–204.

88. Reid, T., *Essays on the Intellectual Powers of*

Man, ed. A. D. Woozley (Macmillan, London, 1941).

89. Reinhardt, L. R., 'Wittgenstein and Strawson on Other Minds', *Studies in the Philosophy of Wittgenstein*, ed. P. Winch (Routledge & Kegan Paul, London, 1969; Humanities Press, New York, 1969) pp. 152–65.

90. Rose, S., *The Conscious Brain* (Weidenfeld & Nicolson, London, 1972).

91. Russell, B., *The Analysis of Mind* (Allen & Unwin, London, 1921).

92. Russell, B., *The Problems of Philosophy* (O.U.P., London, 1912).

93. Ryle, G., *The Concept of Mind*, Hutchinson University Library (Hutchinson, London, 1949).

94. Schlick, M., 'Meaning and Verification', *Philosophical Review*, 45 (1936) pp. 339–69.

95 Scott, W. H., 'Consciousness and Self-Consciousness', *Philosophical Review*, 27 (1918) pp. 1–20.

96. Shaffer, J., 'Persons and their Bodies', *Philosophical Review*, 25 (1966) pp. 59–77.

97. Shoemaker, S., 'Memory', *Encyclopedia of Philosophy*, ed. P. Edwards (The Macmillan Co. of New York and Free Press, New York, 1967) vol. 5, 265–74.

98. Shoemaker, S., 'On Knowing Who One Is', *Common Factor*, 4 (Autumn 1966) pp. 49–56.

99. Shoemaker, S., 'Personal Identity and Memory', *Journal of Philosophy*, 56 (1959) pp. 868–82.

100. Shoemaker, S., *Self-Knowledge and Self-Identity* (Cornell University Press, New York, 1963).

101. Shoemaker, S., 'Self-Reference and Self-Awareness', *Journal of Philosophy*, 65 (1968) pp. 555–67.

102. Shoemaker, S., 'Wiggins on Identity', *Philosophical Review*, 78 (1970) pp. 529–44.

103. Shorter, J. M., 'Personal Identity, Personal Relationships and Criteria', *Proceedings Aristotelian Society*, 71 (1970–1) pp. 165–86

104. Smith, N. K., *Philosophy of David Hume* (Macmillan, London, 1949).
105. Stevenson, I., *Twenty Cases Suggestive of Reincarnation*, Proceedings of the American Society for Psychical Research, 26, (1966).
106. Strawson, P. F., *Individuals* (Methuen, London, 1959).
107. Vesey, G., 'Other Minds', *Understanding Wittgenstein*, Royal Institute of Philosophy Lectures, 7, 1972–3 (Macmillan, London, 1974) pp. 149–61.
108. Wells, H. G., *The Short Stories of H. G. Wells* (Benn, London, 1927).
109. White, R., 'Can Whether One Proposition Makes Sense Depend on the Truth of Another? (*Tractatus*, 2.0211–2)', *Understanding Wittgenstein*, Royal Institute of Philosophy Lectures, 7, 1972–3 (Macmillan, London, 1974) pp. 14–29.
110. Wiggins, D., *Identity and Spatio-temporal Continuity* (Basil Blackwell, Oxford, 1967).
111. Williams, B., 'Bodily Continuity and Personal Identity – a Reply', *Analysis*, 21 (1961) pp. 43–8.
112. Williams, B., *Imagination and the Self* (British Academy, London, 1966).
113. Williams, B., 'Personal Identity and Individuation', *Proceedings Aristotelian Society*, 57 (1956–7) pp. 229–52.
114. Williams, B., 'The Self and the Future', *Philosophical Review*, 79 (1970) pp. 161–80.
115. Wittgenstein, L., 'Notes for Lectures on "Private Experience" and "Sense Data" ', *Philosophical Review*, 77 (1968) pp. 271–320.
116. Wittgenstein, L., *Philosophische Bemerkungen* (Basil Blackwell, Oxford, 1964).
117. Wittgenstein, L., *Philosophical Investigations* (Basil Blackwell, Oxford, 1953).
118. Wittgenstein, L., *The Blue and Brown Books* (Basil Blackwell, Oxford, 1958).
119. Wittgenstein, L., *Tractatus Logico-Philosophicus* (Kegan Paul, London, 1922).

120. Wittgenstein, L., *Zettel* (Basil Blackwell, Oxford, 1967).
121. Woodhouse, M. B., 'Selves and Minds: a Reply to Prof. Knox', *Religious Studies*, 6 (1970) pp. 263–72.
122. Wright, J. W., 'Self-Identity', *Aristotelian Society Supplementary Volume*, 18 (1939) pp. 1–30.

INDEX

Library of Congress Cataloging in Publication Data
(For Library Cataloging Purposes Only)

Vesey, Godfrey Norman Agmondisham.
    Personal identity.

    Reprint of the 1974 ed. published by Macmillan, London, in
    series: Problems of philosophy.
    Bibliography: p.
    Includes index.
    1. Hume, David, 1711-1776. 2. Self (Philosophy) 3. Per-
    sonality. I. Title
[B1499.S45V47 1976]   126′.092′4   76-41208
ISBN 0–8014–9162–2